GREEK WITH GUSTO!

Greek Cuisine — Easy & Delicious

NICHOLAS AND JULIE ROUKES

**Dedicated to the Greek gusto:
The celebration of health,
good humor and philoxenia.**

With philoxenia and Gusto!

Dick and Julie Roukes

FRONT COVER —
Souvlaki (Souvlakia), page 125
Greek Salad (Salata Horiatiki), page 18

JUNIRO ARTS PUBLICATIONS, CALGARY

ACKNOWLEDGEMENTS: The authors are grateful to Mrs. Nota Solomos, home economist, for proofreading the manuscript and contributing several recipes. They also wish to thank Mrs. Helen Vlahos, president of *The Daughters of Penelope,* Calgary Chapter and Michelle Iatrou, for their support and are particularly grateful to Margo Embury of Centax for invaluable assistance in book editing, designing and food styling.

GREEK with GUSTO!
by
Nicholas Roukes & Julie Roukes

First Printing - May 1990

Copyright © 1990 Nicholas Roukes and Julie Roukes.
JUNIRO ARTS PUBLICATIONS
28 Butte Place NW
Calgary, Alberta, Canada
T2L 1P2

Canadian Cataloguing in Publication Data

Roukes, Nicholas
   Greek with gusto!

   ISBN: 0-919845-80-0

1. Cookery, Greek.   I. Roukes, Julie.   II. Title.
TX723.5.G8R68 1990   641.59495   C90-097089-8

Photography and drawings by Nicholas Roukes

Dishes and accessories courtesy of:
Benkris & Co.
Mount Royal Village
Calgary, Alberta

Marcelle's
1126-17th Avenue S.W.
Calgary, Alberta

Designed, Printed and Produced in Canada by:
Centax Books, a Division of M.C. Graphics Inc.
Publishing Director and Food Stylist: Margo Embury
1048 Fleury Street, Regina, Saskatchewan, Canada S4N 4W8
(306) 359-3737 / 359-7580   FAX (306) 525-3955

CONTENTS

INTRODUCTION

❦

"What I eat I turn into work and good humor."
— *Zorba the Greek*

❦

Whether in song, dance or food, Greeks love to share their joyful spirit. Their friendliness and open-hearted generosity to strangers is known as *Philoxenia.*

In that same spirit, we wish to share with you the legendary Greek cuisine. We think you'll agree that GREEK WITH GUSTO! aspires to being more than a mere ethnic cookbook but rather, a celebration of generous, full-flavored cooking which is concerned with health and fitness and — because of its myriad and wonderful ways of combining foods, herbs and spices — a provider of great comfort and satisfaction to both body and soul.

Here, you'll find recipes for dishes for every course and every meal with robust, vibrant flavor, ranging from tempting appetizers, savory pites, wholesome and delicious soups and stews, sumptuous main courses, to delectable desserts that add a perfect finishing touch to any meal.

The Greek cook's emphasis on simply prepared foods remains virtually unchanged since the time of Archestratus who wrote the first cookbook over 2000 years ago. Because Greek cuisine stems from a history of many centuries of culinary practice, it has — like a good stew — simmered slowly to become a world-class foodfare. The recipes in this book have evolved from a long lineage of great cooks which include Greek mothers, grandmothers, chefs and restauranteurs — each one adding his or her special touch to perfect the "Golden Oldie" recipes, while at the same time, adding new touches to extend the genius of the time-honored cuisine.

We have enjoyed travelling throughout Greece and its islands seeking and collecting culinary treasures to add to those already in our repertoire. And, of course, we've taken great delight in cooking and testing the recipes, modifying many to meet requirements of being lower in calories and saturated fats in keeping with today's nutritional standards, yet making sure they preserve the goodness and flavor that made them famous. The good news is that judicious Greek cooking, prepared mainly with monounsaturated olive oil (which is beneficial to good health) can actually help keep cholesterol levels low over a long period of time — a fact that appears to have been known to the Greek civilization for centuries.

Conveniently, many of the recipes in this book are easy-to-prepare casserole meals — luxurious one-dish dazzlers that cook virtually unattended on the rangetop or in the oven. They are good "keepers" too, usually developing an even fuller and more robust flavor the day after they are cooked — ideal for large families, professional working couples or anyone who seeks to avoid the panic of last minute cooking.

So, go GREEK with GUSTO! Prepare these savory meals, treat your family and friends, then sit back and enjoy the compliments. We'll be wishing you success, good health and, as they say in Greece — *KALI OREXI! Bon appétit!*

Nicholas and Julie Roukes

Legend has it that Greek food is so delicious, even the cooking aromas can cause one to swoon in ecstacy. Translated, IMAM BAILDI (a baked eggplant tomato casserole), means "The priest fainted."

Greek With Gusto!

APPETIZERS
Mezethes

Serving *Mezethes* is a sign of hospitality — and a great way to welcome your guests. *Mezethes* — the Greek word for appetizers — may consist of wedges of Greek cheese, black olives, Greek meatballs, kalamarakia, savory pites, crusty bread, a small portion of one's favorite casserole served cold or any of the entrées described in APPETIZERS or SAVORY PITES. In Greece, appetizers are served either as a prelude to dinner or as a snack to accompany an ouzo. Although you may serve a platter of these delicious morsels as a complete meal, remember that as a first course, they are intended to whet the appetite, not spoil it!

TZATZIKI

Tzatziki
MAKES ABOUT 4 SERVINGS

This yogurt-cucumber sauce is delicious as a dip, or as an accompaniment for cooked vegetables, meat, or fish.

1	**large cucumber, peeled and minced or grated and drained**	1
2 cups	**plain yogurt**	500 mL
3	**garlic cloves, crushed through a press or 4 green onions, chopped**	4
	salt and pepper	

Combine all ingredients in a glass bowl. Mix well and refrigerate. Serve cold.

NOTE: To make an extra-thick sauce, use the richest yogurt available. Place in a cheesecloth-lined sieve over a bowl. Do not stir. Let the yogurt drain overnight at room temperature.

HUMUS

Revithia Tahini
MAKES ABOUT 2 CUPS

The happy marriage of chickpeas and tahini provides a wonderful flavor for this dip or spread. Tahini is a sesame paste available from Greek groceries or Middle-Eastern food stores.

19 oz.	**can chickpeas, drained**	540 mL
3 tsp.	**tahini**	15 mL
3	**garlic cloves, minced**	3
3 tbsp.	**chopped, fresh parsley**	45 mL
¼ cup	**olive oil**	50 mL
1	**lemon, juice of**	1
½ tsp.	**ground coriander**	2 mL
½ tsp.	**ground cumin**	2 mL
	salt and pepper	

Combine all the ingredients in a food processor or blender. Process until ingredients form a smooth paste.

TARAMOSALATA

Taramosalata
MAKES ABOUT 2 CUPS

T ARAMOSALATA is made with TARAMA (carp roe caviar), available from Greek stores. You'll love it as a spread or dip.

1 cup	mashed potatoes	250 mL
4	slices white bread, crusts removed	4
4 oz.	tarama	113 g
1	small onion, coarsely chopped	1
1 cup	olive oil	250 mL
1½	lemons, juice of	1½

Combine all of the ingredients in a food processor. Process until a smooth thick consistencey is formed and serve.

NOTE: Thin with yogurt or sour cream for a salad dressing.

SKORDALIA

Skordalia
MAKES 2 CUPS

A delightful garlic dip for bread sticks and crackers. Try it as an accompaniment for fish and vegetables.

5	slices thickly-sliced white bread, crusts removed	5
⅔ cup	water	150 mL
6	garlic cloves, coarsely chopped	6
½ cup	blanched, whole almonds	125 mL
⅓ cup	lemon juice	75 mL
⅔ cup	olive oil	150 mL
	salt	

Cut bread into quarters, place in a bowl and sprinkle with water. Allow to stand for 10 minutes. Combine garlic and almonds in a food processor. Process until fairly smooth. Add bread, lemon juice, olive oil and salt. Continue to process until a thick, creamy consistency is obtained. If necessary, thin with water and/or lemon juice. To thicken, add more bread and process a few seconds longer. Serve chilled.

EGGPLANT DIP

Melitzanosalata

MAKES ABOUT 2 CUPS

This eggplant purée — often called "the peasant's caviar" — is wonderful as a dip or spread.

1	medium eggplant, halved	1
3 tbsp.	olive oil	45 mL
1	small onion, finely chopped	1
2	garlic cloves, minced	2
¼ cup	chopped, fresh parsley	50 mL
	salt and pepper	
¼ cup	chopped pimientos	50 mL
½ cup	toasted pine nuts (optional)	125 mL

Brush the eggplant halves with 1 tbsp. (15 mL) olive oil. Place on a baking sheet, cut-side-down. Bake in a 350°F (180°C) oven for 45 minutes or until tender. Cool, scoop out pulp, and reserve.

Sauté onion and garlic in remaining olive oil until onion is tender. Place eggplant pulp in food processor, along with sautéed onion and garlic, parsley, salt and pepper. Process for a few seconds until smooth. Transfer the mixture to a bowl and stir in pimientos. Refrigerate for several hours or overnight to allow development of full flavor. Bring to room temperature before serving. Stir in toasted pine nuts if desired.

NOTES: Cubed eggplant may be microwaved with 2 tbsp. (30 mL) of water in a covered bowl. Microwave for 9 minutes on HIGH (9) or until tender. Drain the eggplant, discard juices and cool. For a smoky flavor, roast the whole eggplant over a gas flame or under a broiler until the skin blackens. Cool, rub off skin, chop, and proceed as above.

SAGANAKI

Saganaki

Fried Greek cheese. What a delightful appetizer! Don't let your guests eat too much, they'll want to make a meal of it.

**graviera, kasseri or kefalotiri
   cheese, cut into ½" (1 cm) slices
flour
butter or margarine
lemon wedges**

Dust the cheese lightly with flour. Heat a skillet over medium-high heat. Add butter and fry the cheese until golden brown on both sides. Transfer to a warm plate, squeeze lemon juice over the slices and serve immediately.

ADD TO THE GUSTO! TO MAKE SAGANAKI FLAMBÉ: Remove skillet from stove, pour a jigger of warmed brandy over the cheese and light with a long matchstick. Serve with lemon wedges when flame subsides.

KALAMARAKIA

Kalamarakia Tiganita

MAKES 4 TO 6 SERVINGS

A popular appetizer found in Greek tavernas. It's easy to make and delicious served with lemon wedges or *Skordalia Sauce.*

2 lbs.	**squid**	1 kg
	salt and pepper	
	olive oil for frying	
	lemon wedges	

Clean squid as directed on page 109 and pat dry. Cut into ¼" (5 mm) rings and season with salt and pepper. Use enough olive oil to cover the bottom of a skillet and fry the squid, in small batches, over high heat for 2 minutes. Drain on paper towel and transfer to a warm plate. Garnish with lemon wedges. Serve immediately with *Skordalia Sauce,* page 9.

Stuffed Grape Leaves

Dolmadakia

MAKES ABOUT 100 DOLMADAKIA

This popular Greek appetizer has become internationally acclaimed. Don't let the length of the recipe deter you from making it. Actually, it's just a series of simple steps and well worth the effort!

16 oz.	jar grape leaves	500 g
¼ cup	olive oil	50 mL
2	large onions, chopped	2
4	garlic cloves, minced	4
1 cup	uncooked long-grain rice	250 mL
1 cup	hot water	250 mL
1	lemon, juice of	1
½ tsp.	sugar	2 mL
¾ cup	chopped dillweed or 1 tbsp. crushed, dry dillweed	175 mL
5 tbsp.	currants, washed and chopped	75 mL
1 tbsp.	olive oil	15 mL
	salt and pepper	
5 tbsp.	pine nuts	75 mL

Remove grape leaves from jar and rinse well. Reserve the thickest and damaged leaves for lining the bottom of the cooking pan. Heat a skillet over medium-high heat. When pan is hot, add ¼ cup (50 mL) olive oil. Sauté onions and garlic until onions are translucent. Stir in rice, hot water, lemon juice, sugar, dillweed, currants, the tablespoon of olive oil, salt and pepper. Mix well, cover and bring to a boil. Reduce heat and simmer for 7 minutes or until juices are absorbed. Remove from heat, cool and stir in pine nuts.

TO ASSEMBLE: Cut off stems from grape leaves. Lay them on a clean surface, dull side up, with stem end facing up. Place 1 tsp. (5 mL) of the rice mixture at the bottom of the leaf as shown. Fold bottom of the leaf over the filling. Fold the sides in towards the middle. Roll into a small oblong shape. The roll should be snug, but loose enough to allow for expansion of the rice as it cooks. Repeat until all dolmadakia are assembled.

STUFFED GRAPE LEAVES

Continued

Layer the dolmadakia seam-side-down in a Dutch oven lined with the thickest and damaged grape leaves or parsley stalks. Place an inverted plate over them to weight them down (and prevent them from opening during cooking). Pour in enough water to just cover the dolmadakia. Heat to the boiling point over medium-high heat, lower heat, cover and simmer for 1 hour or until tender. Remove from heat, cool and refrigerate. Serve cold on cocktail picks, or warm with *Avgolemono Sauce,* page 137, as a main course.

NOTE: Lining the pan with grape leaves prevents the dolmadakia from burning or sticking to the pan.

ADD TO THE GUSTO! TO MAKE MEAT-STUFFED DOLMADAKIA: Use only ½ cup (125 mL) rice, add 1 pound (500 g) lean ground beef and sauté with the onions. Proceed as directed above. Omit lemon juice.

See photograph page 33.

  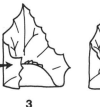

1   2   3   4   5

SPICY PORK MEATBALLS

Loukanika

MAKES ABOUT 50 MEATBALLS

These spicy meatballs are very Greek. Orange zest, herbs and spices provide a wonderful accent.

1½ lbs.	pork shoulder butt steak, coarsely ground	750 g
½ cup	fine bread crumbs	125 mL
½ cup	dry white wine	125 mL
1	orange, grated zest of	1
1 tsp.	crushed, dry marjoram	5 mL
1 tsp.	crushed, dry savory	5 mL
1 tsp.	cinnamon	5 mL
1 tsp.	allspice	5 mL
2	garlic cloves, crushed through a press or minced	2
	salt and pepper	
2 tbsp.	olive oil	30 mL
	lemon wedges for garnish	

Place all of the ingredients except oil and lemon in a large bowl and mix thoroughly, kneading with hands. Cover tightly and refrigerate overnight, allowing flavors to blend and permeate the meat. Form the mixture into walnut-sized balls. Fry in olive oil until brown on all sides or place in a single layer in a slightly oiled shallow baking pan and bake in a 500°F (260°C) oven for 10 minutes. Serve hot on cocktail picks, garnished with lemon wedges.

NOTE: An alternate way to use this recipe: Form the meat into patties. Grill, broil or fry them. Serve in a bun, hamburger style, along with your favorite trimmings.

GREEK MEATBALLS

Keftedakia

MAKES ABOUT 50 MEATBALLS

Hot or cold, these little morsels are divine! If you're so inclined, try them with a glass of ouzo. After all, it was Archestratus who said, "Eat while you drink, because this is the way cultured people should live!"

1½ lbs.	ground meat (beef, lamb or pork)	750 g
1	medium onion, finely chopped	1
2	garlic cloves, crushed through a press or minced	2
½ cup	bread crumbs	125 mL
1	egg, lightly beaten	1
3 tbsp.	chopped mint or 1 tsp. (5 mL) crushed, dry mint	45 mL
½ tsp.	crushed, dry oregano salt and pepper flour for dredging	2 mL
2 tbsp.	olive oil	30 mL

Place the meat in a mixing bowl. Add onion, garlic, bread crumbs, egg, mint, oregano, salt and pepper. Knead the mixture thoroughly. Shape into 1" (2.5 cm) balls. Spread flour lightly on wax paper, roll meatballs over flour to cover lightly. Fry in a skillet in olive oil over medium-high heat until the meatballs are evenly browned.

NOTE: TO BAKE THE MEATBALLS: Do not roll in flour. Place meatballs in a single layer in a shallow baking pan. Bake in a 500°F (260°C) oven for 10 minutes or until brown. Turning is unnecessary.

See photograph page 33.

"I at last realized that eating was a spiritual function and that meat, bread and wine were the raw materials from which the mind is made."
— *Zorba the Greek*

FRIED LIVER

Sikotakia Tiganita
MAKES 6 SERVINGS

We loved this the very first time we tasted it in a Greek taverna. It may be made from calf, lamb or chicken livers.

1 lb.	liver, cut into bite-size pieces	500 g
4 tbsp.	olive oil or butter	60 mL
	salt and pepper	
	oregano, crushed, dry	
	lemon wedges for garnish	

Rinse liver and pat dry. Freeze briefly to facilitate subsequent cutting. Cut into bite-sized pieces. In a frying pan, sauté quickly over medium-high heat in oil or butter. Arrange on a platter, season with oregano, salt and freshly ground pepper. Spear with cocktail picks. Garnish with lemon wedges and serve immediately.

OVEN FRIES

Patates Psites Fournou
MAKES 6 SERVINGS

Fries with a difference! Enjoy these scrumptious low-fat oven-fried potatoes with *Tzatziki Sauce,* page 8.

6	medium-size new white potatoes	6
¼ cup	olive oil	50 mL
	oregano, crushed, dry	
	salt to taste	
	garlic powder	

Preheat the oven to 375°F (190°C). Warm baking sheets in the oven while preparing the potatoes. Wash and dry potatoes. It is not necessary to peel them. Cut potatoes into finger shapes, approximately 3" x ½" x ½" (7 cm x 1 cm x 1 cm). Toss with oil in a large bowl. Arrange potatoes on the baking sheets in a single layer. Bake for 15 minutes, turn, and bake for an additional 10 minutes or until tender. Remove from the oven and place in a paper bag. Sprinkle oregano, salt and garlic powder into the bag, shake gently, and serve.

VEGETABLE PATTIES

Kolokithokeftedes

MAKES ABOUT 12 PATTIES

You can easily make a complete meal of these "veggie-burgers"! Great as an appetizer, side dish, or as a brunch specialty. We love them in pita bread, along with a dollop of *Tzatziki Sauce,* page 8, sliced tomatoes and leafy lettuce.

3 cups	grated zucchini	750 mL
1	medium onion, finely chopped	1
2	garlic cloves, minced	2
½ cup	chopped, fresh parsley	125 mL
2	eggs, beaten	2
1 cup	bread crumbs	250 mL
3 tbsp.	crumbled feta or grated kasseri or Parmesan	45 mL
	salt and pepper	
2 tbsp.	olive oil	30 mL
	flour for dredging	

Wash and grate zucchini. Wrap in several layers of cheesecloth and squeeze out juice. In a bowl, combine zucchini with remaining ingredients except for olive oil and flour. Shape into medium-small patties. Dredge lightly in flour. Fry in hot oil in a skillet until golden brown. Drain on paper towel. Keep warm in the oven until all the patties are cooked. Serve hot with either yogurt, *Tzatziki,* or sour cream.

NOTE: The zucchini mixture may be formed into small "meatballs", speared with cocktail picks and served as appetizers.

GREEK SALAD

Salata Horiatiki

MAKES 4 TO 6 SERVINGS

This traditional Greek villager's salad is a visual treat as well as a tasty low-calorie delight.

4	medium-sized ripe tomatoes, cut in wedges	4
2	cucumbers, peeled, halved, and cut into thick slices	2
1	small red or white onion, thinly sliced	1
20	Kalamata olives	20
	crumbled oregano	
	salt and pepper	
2 tbsp.	olive oil	30 mL
¾ cup	crumbled feta cheese	175 mL
	olives for garnish	

In a large shallow serving dish, combine tomatoes, cucumbers, onion, and olives. Sprinkle with oregano, salt and pepper; drizzle with olive oil and toss. Sprinkle feta over salad. Garnish with additional olives.

ADD TO THE GUSTO! Other ingredients to be added to GREEK SALAD include: Sliced red, yellow or green bell peppers; sliced lettuce or other greens; diced celery, capers, green peas, anchovies or cooked and cubed potatoes.

AN ALTERNATE GREEK SALAD DRESSING:

2	parts olive oil	2
1	part lemon juice or wine vinegar	1
½ tsp.	sugar	2 mL
1	garlic clove, crushed through a press or minced	1
	salt and pepper	
	oregano, crushed, dry	

Combine all ingredients in a small jar and shake. Drizzle over salad just before serving.

See photograph on front cover.

OLIVES AND CHEESES

GREEK OLIVES (Elies)

Olives are everpresent at the Greek table. Perhaps the most popular are the blackish-purple *Kalamata Olives* from the Peloponnesos which are brine-cured and packed in vinegar. Other types include *Amphissa,* the large, black, juicy olives from central Greece; *Black Olives,* the commonly grown small, round, wrinkled and slightly bitter olives, and the oblong-shaped *Agrinion,* which are green, smooth-skinned and have a slightly bitter taste.

GREEK CHEESES (Tiria)

Greek cheeses are delicious in cooking, as seasoning for sauces, in salads, and as appetizers. Some of the most popular and more widely available Greek cheeses include:

FETA: A white, semisoft and flaky cheese made from goat's or sheep's milk which is salted and packed in brine. Feta is commonly eaten sliced as a table cheese. It is excellent in salads or for use in cooking.

KASSERI: A mild-flavored cheese that is creamy in color and Cheddar-like in texture. It is one of the most popular table cheeses.

KEFALOTIRI: A hard, salty, pale yellow cheese used mostly for grating over pastas, baking in casseroles and sprinkling into pites.

GRAVIERA or KEFALOGRAVIERA: A Gruyère-type cheese that may be used for grating and serving with pasta or eaten as a table cheese. An excellent choice for making *Saganaki,* page 11.

MIZITHRA: Used either as a table cheese or for making sweet and savory pites. There are two types: The soft, unsalted type which is useful for making pites, and the semihard, lightly salted type used as a table or grating cheese. Cottage cheese or ricotta may be substituted for the soft mizithra.

MANOURI: A soft, white, unsalted cheese that is similar to the soft mizithra. It is commonly used for making sweet or savory pites or eaten as a table cheese.

*Contemporary food writers note
that the art of cookery has united
the old world with the new.*

PHYLLO SAVORIES
Pites

*P*ITES, *pronounced Pea-tez,* or *Pita* (singular), are savory food "pies" made with PHYLLO (or FILO), pronounced *feel-o,* paper-thin pastry sheets available from Greek grocery stores and supermarkets. These pastry sheets are used in four different ways to make pites in the form of TRIANGLES, ROLL-UPS, PURSES or IN-THE-PAN. In each instance, food is encased within the pastry to produce tasty delights such as: SPANAKOPITA (spinach-filled pita), TIROPITA (cheese-filled), KREATOPITA (meat-filled), KOTOPITA (with chicken), PSAROPITA (seafood), and HORTOPITA (vegetable-filled). You'll find recipes for these and other classic savory pies in the pages that follow.

FOUR WAYS TO MAKE GREEK PITES

1. **TRIANGLES (Trigona)**
2. **ROLL-UPS (Bourekakia)**
3. **"PURSES" (Portofolia)**
4. **IN-THE-PAN (Pita Tapsiou)**

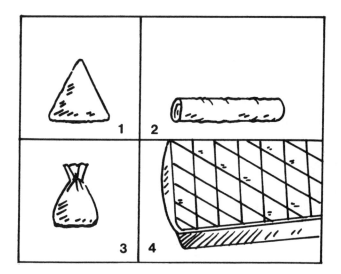

BASIC KITCHEN NEEDS TO MAKE GREEK PITES

Baking pans, phyllo sheets, damp cloth, pastry brush, kitchen knife, scissors, melted butter, food mixture.

ABOUT PHYLLO

You'll find phyllo in the frozen food section in most supermarkets or ethnic specialty stores. The frozen phyllo is packaged in one-pound boxes which contain from 20 - 30 pastry sheets measuring about 14" x 17" (35.5 cm x 43 cm). Be sure to thaw frozen phyllo 24 hours in the refrigerator prior to use.

NOTES: Use fresh phyllo if available or freshly thawed phyllo; it's much easier to handle, does not have ragged edges, and doesn't break apart when lifted. Remove phyllo from the package only when ready to use. Unroll the sheets on a flat, dry surface and cover with a slightly dampened cloth to protect them from drying out. Uncover only when removing each sheet. If the edges of the phyllo show premature drying, mist lightly with water. You may brush pites with melted margarine or olive oil rather than butter. Pites may be stored in the refrigerator 2 to 3 days before baking and can go directly into the oven from the refrigerator.

STORING AND FREEZING PITES: Pites may be frozen either before or after baking. They will keep in the freezer for 2 to 3 months. When ready to bake, thaw 45 minutes and bake slightly longer than the time specified in the recipe.

RECRISPING PITES: Pites that have been baked and refrigerated should be recrisped by placing them in a 300°F (150°C) oven for a few minutes prior to serving.

WHAT TO DO WITH LEFTOVER PHYLLO? Use it to make scrumptious pastry desserts in the form of triangles, roll-ups or purses, see illustration. Fill with a mixture of sliced apple, raisins, sugar and cinnamon and bake as directed for savory pites.

CLARIFIED BUTTER (salt and milk solids removed) produces a crisper, flakier pita: Microwave butter on high for 2 minutes. Skim solids from the top and use the clear clarified butter in the center. Discard solids at the bottom. For stovetop directions, see page 145.

PITES

HOW TO MAKE TRIANGLE PITES *(Trigona)*

Thaw frozen phyllo in the refrigerator for 24 hours before use. Remove phyllo from the package, unroll, and lay it flat on the counter. Cover with a slightly dampened tea towel. Remove 1 sheet of phyllo and cut into 4 equal-sized strips. Take 2 of the strips, (cover the other two temporarily), brush with melted butter, and place on top of each other. Place 1 tsp. (5 mL) of food mixture at the bottom end as shown in figure 2. Lift the corner of the filo so that it forms a right triangle. Continue to fold until a triangle-shaped pita is created as in figure 5. Repeat procedure until required number of triangles are formed. Brush each triangle, top and bottom, with butter and set on a baking sheet, seam-side down. It is not necessary to grease the baking sheet. With the tip of a sharp knife, pierce each pita 2 or 3 times to allow steam to escape during baking. Sprinkle with a few drops of water to prevent curling of top layers and encourage even browning. Bake in a preheated 350°F (180°C) oven for 20 minutes or until golden brown.

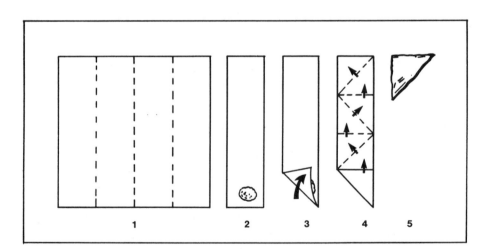

PITES

HOW TO MAKE ROLL-UP PITES *(Bourekakia)*

Allow phyllo pastry sheets to thaw in the refrigerator for 24 hours before using. Remove phyllo from the package, unroll and lay flat on the counter. Cover with a slightly dampened tea towel. Remove 1 sheet at a time and cut in half lengthways. Keep one half on the counter, place the other half with the unused sheets under the damp cloth. (To prevent drying out). Brush half of the pastry strip with melted butter, fold in half, and brush with more melted butter. Spread 1 tbsp. (15 mL) of filling along the bottom edge. Fold the right and left edges of the phyllo in about ½" (1 cm) as shown in figure 3. Brush sides with butter and roll up to make a tight roll, brushing with butter as you go. Be sure the entire surface is brushed with melted butter. Place on an ungreased baking sheet, seam-side down. Repeat the procedure until all the rolls have been made. Pierce each roll 2 or 3 times with the tip of a sharp knife. Sprinkle lightly with a few drops of water. Bake in the center of a 350°F (180°C) oven for 20 minutes or until crisp and golden.

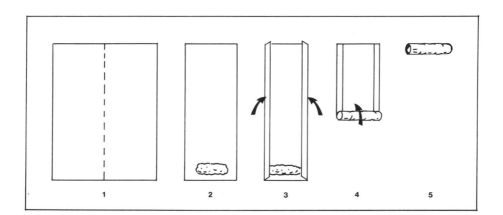

PITES

HOW TO MAKE PURSES *(Portofolia)*

Allow phyllo to thaw in the refrigerator for 24 hours before using. Remove phyllo from the package, unroll and lay flat on the counter. Cover with a slightly dampened tea towel. Remove 1 sheet of phyllo, brush lightly with melted butter. Place a second sheet of phyllo over it and again brush with melted butter. With a sharp knife, cut into 6 equal-sized squares measuring 5" x 5" (12.7 x 12.7 cm). Place approximately 1 tbsp. (15 mL) of food mixture in the center of each square. Pick up the corners of the phyllo and bring together over the top. Gently twist the gathered portions to form a pouch. Pinch the neck of the twisted top tightly to ensure a seal. If phyllo is dry, moisten finger tips with water to make a tighter seal. Brush each "little purse" with melted butter and set on baking sheet. Sprinkle with a few drops of water. Bake in a preheated 350°F (180°C) oven for 15 minutes or until golden.

HOW TO MAKE PITA-IN-THE-PAN *(Pita Tapsiou)*

Allow phyllo to thaw in the refrigerator for 24 hours before using. Remove phyllo from the package, unroll and lay flat on the counter. Cut the phyllo sheets so they are the exact size of the pan. Stack and cover with a slightly dampened cloth. Butter the sides and bottom of a rectangular baking pan. Place 1 sheet of phyllo on the bottom of the pan. Brush lightly with melted butter. Lay a second sheet of phyllo over it, and brush again with butter. Repeat until 8 sheets of phyllo have been layered and buttered. Spread the food mixture evenly over the top layer. Cover the food mixture with 10 to 12 additional layers of phyllo, brushing each lightly with melted butter. With a sharp knife, cut into diamond or square shapes as shown in the illustration. Sprinkle with a few drops of water. Bake in a preheated 350°F (180°C) oven for 45 minutes or until golden.

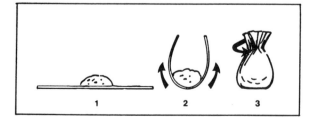

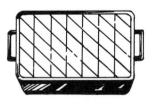

SPINACH-RICE PITA

Spanakorizopita
MAKES ABOUT 40 TRIANGLES

Method: Triangles

A wonderful innovation: Spinach-rice pilaf, wrapped in phyllo pastry! Yia-Yia (grandmother) would prepare this to get her family to eat spinach. Now they can't get enough of the stuff!

2 cups	spanakorizo, page 59	500 mL
1 cup	crumbled feta	250 mL
1 lb.	phyllo pastry	454 g
1 cup	melted butter or margarine	250 mL

TO PREPARE FILLING: Make spanakorizo according to directions on page 59. Allow to cool and toss with crumbled feta. Set aside.

Prepare and fill phyllo triangles according to directions on page 24. Brush each triangle, top and bottom, with melted butter and place on an ungreased baking sheet. Pierce with the tip of a knife and sprinkle with a few drops of water. Bake in a preheated 350°F (180°C) oven for 20 minutes or until golden brown.

❧

FILÓ, PHÝLLO or FÍLOS. Depending on where you put the accent, these sound alikes have entirely different meanings. FILÓ means I KISS, PHÝLLO means LEAF, and FÍLOS means FRIEND. Confused? Perhaps that's why some say, "It's all Greek to me!"

❧

SPINACH PITA

Spanakopita
Method: In-the-pan
MAKES ABOUT 14 SERVINGS

Everybody loves spinach when it's made like this! Spanakopita is a wonderful layered dish comprised of spinach, cheese and pastry. It's equally delicious served hot or cold.

2	bunches fresh spinach or 2 x 10 oz. (454 g) packages frozen, thawed, drained	2
1 cup	crumbled feta	250 mL
4 oz.	cream cheese	125 g
1 cup	dry curd cottage cheese	250 mL
6	eggs, separated	6
12	green onions, finely chopped and lightly sautéed	12
3 tbsp.	chopped dill or mint or 2 tsp. (10 mL) crushed, dry dillweed or mint	45 mL
	salt and pepper	
1 lb.	phyllo sheets	454 g
1 cup	melted butter or margarine	250 mL

TO MAKE THE FILLING: Wash spinach thoroughly. Place in a saucepan with only the water that clings to the leaves and cook over medium-low heat for 3 minutes or until the leaves are wilted. Cool, squeeze dry, chop and place in a bowl. Add feta, softened cream cheese, cottage cheese, egg yolks, green onions, dillweed or mint, salt and pepper. Mix well. Beat the egg whites until stiff and fold into the mixture.

TO ASSEMBLE: Butter a shallow rectangular pan. Lay 8 phyllo sheets into the pan, 1 at a time, brushing each with melted butter. Spread the spinach mixture over the top layer. Lay an additional 8 to 10 sheets of phyllo over the mixture, brushing each sheet with butter. With a sharp knife, cut into diamond or square shapes. Bake in a preheated 350°F (180°C) oven for 1 hour or until golden brown. Allow to cool slightly and serve.

NOTES: A time-saving hint: Place spinach in a glass bowl with just the water that clings to the leaves. Cover and microwave on HIGH (9) for 3 minutes.

See photograph page 33.

Vegetarian Pita

Hortopita

Method: Triangles

MAKES ABOUT 40 TRIANGLES

This delicious pita is made by combining a fresh garden green such as chard, spinach, endive, leafy lettuce, fiddleheads, dandelion greens or sorrel with semisoft Greek *mizithra* cheese and Yogurt-Onion Sauce.

2	bunches green chard	2
1½ cups	grated mizithra cheese	375 mL
½ cup	toasted pine nuts	125 mL
¼ tsp.	grated nutmeg	1 mL
	salt and pepper	
1 cup	Yogurt-Onion Sauce, page 37	250 mL
1 lb.	phyllo pastry	454 g
1 cup	melted butter or margarine	250 mL

Wash greens thoroughly. Remove tough stems, tear into pieces and cook in a small amount of water for 8 to 10 minutes or until tender. You can microwave greens in a covered bowl on HIGH (9) with only the water clinging to the leaves for 3 to 5 minutes, turning the bowl once. Drain well and set aside to cool. In a bowl, mix greens, cheese, pine nuts, nutmeg, salt, pepper and Yogurt-Onion Sauce. Proceed with directions to make phyllo triangles as described on page 24. Bake in a preheated 350°F (180°C) oven for 20 minutes or until golden brown. Serve warm or cold.

❦

Set yourself after the ancient Greeks because they are the rule of beauty, and give us a good gusto.
— Dryden

❦

ZUCCHINI PITA

Kolokithopita

Method: In-The-Pan

MAKES ABOUT 6 SERVINGS

Aside from zucchini, any type of summer or winter squash such as straight neck, yellow crooked neck, butternut, acorn, Hubbard or turban may be used to make this delicious vegetarian pita.

2 tbsp.	olive oil	30 mL
1	medium onion, finely chopped	1
3	garlic cloves, minced	3
3	medium zucchini, finely diced	3
1 cup	cooked Bulgur Pilaf (processed cracked wheat), page 82	250 mL
2	eggs, lightly beaten	2
²⁄₃ cup	chopped, fresh parsley	150 mL
²⁄₃ cup	toasted pine nuts	150 mL
	freshly ground pepper	
1 cup	crumbled feta	250 mL
1 lb.	phyllo pastry	454 g
1 cup	melted butter or margarine	250 mL

Heat a skillet over medium-high heat. Add olive oil, onion, garlic, zucchini and sauté until onion is soft and translucent. Transfer to a bowl and allow to cool. Stir in Bulgur, eggs, parsley, pine nuts, pepper and feta. Mix well and set aside.

TO ASSEMBLE: Butter a shallow rectangular pan measuring approximately 9" x 13" x 2" (23 cm x 33 cm x 5 cm). Lay 8 phyllo sheets into the pan, 1 at a time, brushing each with melted butter. Spread the zucchini mixture over the top layer. Lay an additional 10 to 12 sheets of phyllo over the mixture, again brushing each sheet with butter. With a sharp knife, cut into diamond or square shapes as shown in figure 4, page 22. Bake in a preheated 350°F (180°C) oven for 45 minutes or until golden brown. Allow to cool slightly and serve.

SKORDOPITA

Skordopita
Method: Triangles
MAKES ABOUT 40 TRIANGLES

A great entrée for the consumate garlic lover. These pites feature *Skordalia,* the famous Greek garlic sauce, as the filling. Try them, they're absolutely delicious!

FILLING

5	**slices thickly-sliced white bread, crust removed**	5
⅔ cup	**water**	150 mL
6	**garlic cloves, coarsley chopped**	6
½ cup	**blanched, whole almonds**	125 mL
⅓ cup	**lemon juice**	75 mL
⅔ cup	**olive oil**	150 mL
	salt	
½ cup	**chopped, fresh parsley**	125 mL
¾ cup	**toasted pine nuts**	175 mL
1 lb.	**phyllo pastry**	454 g
1 cup	**melted butter or margarine**	250 mL

TO PREPARE FILLING: Remove crust from bread and cut into quarters. Place in a bowl and sprinkle with water. Allow to stand for 10 minutes. Combine garlic and almonds in a food processor. Process until fairly smooth. Add bread, lemon juice, olive oil, and salt. Continue to process until a thick, creamy consistency is obtained. Stir in parsley and pine nuts. Makes about 2 cups (500 mL) of filling.

Assemble phyllo triangles as directed on page 24. Bake in a preheated 375°F (190°C) oven for 15 minutes or until golden brown. Cool slightly and serve.

❧

"It is pleasant to change to different foods, for when one is stuffed too often with common viands the mere taste of something new affords redoubled pleasure."
— Antiphanes

❧

LENTIL PURSES

Portofolia Fakies

Method: Purses

MAKES ABOUT 60 PURSES

These delightfully-shaped pites are made of savory lentil purée. Fun to eat — and very nourishing.

1¼ cups	lentils	300 mL
4 cups	water	1 L
1	large onion, chopped	1
6	garlic cloves, minced	6
2	egg yolks, beaten	2
⅔ cup	bread crumbs	150 mL
½ cup	chopped, fresh parsley	125 mL
3 tsp.	ground cumin	15 mL
2 tsp.	ground coriander	10 mL
¼ cup	olive oil	50 mL
1 tbsp.	lemon juice	15 mL
1	small cucumber, peeled, seeded and finely chopped	1
1 lb.	phyllo pastry	454 g
1 cup	melted butter or margarine	250 mL

Wash and rinse lentils. Place in a saucepan, add water and cook, covered, for about 30 minutes. Lentils should be tender but not mushy. Add more water as needed. During the last 10 minutes of cooking, add onion and garlic. Drain, and allow to cool slightly. Place lentil mixture in a processor or blender and process until just smooth. Transfer mixture to a bowl and stir in beaten yolks, bread crumbs, parsley, cumin, coriander, olive oil, lemon juice and cucumber. Mix well. The mixture may be refrigerated, covered, for up to 3 days if you wish to make this recipe in 2 stages.

Assemble purses as directed on page 26. Bake in a preheated 350°F (180°C) oven for 15 minutes or until golden brown. May be served warm or cold.

See photograph opposite.

APPETIZERS —

Lentil Purses (Portofolia Fakies), page 32
Spinach Pita (Spanakopita), page 28
Cheese Rolls (Bourekakia Tiri), page 36
Chicken Pita (Kotopita), page 39
Greek Coffee (Kafes), page 161
Greek Meatballs (Keftedakia), page 15
Stuffed Grape Leaves (Dolmadakia), page 12
Greek Cookies (Koulourakia), page 152
Kalamata Olives & Feta Cheese, page 19

CHEESE PITA

Tiropita

Method: Triangles

MAKES ABOUT 40 TRIANGLES

These crispy golden triangles are absolutely scrumptious as an appetizer or light meal. Serve with white wine, along with Kalamata olives and sliced tomatoes drizzled with olive oil.

1½ cups	crumbled feta	375 mL
1 cup	cottage cheese	250 mL
2	egg yolks, lightly beaten	2
½ cup	chopped, fresh parsley	125 mL
1 tsp.	grated nutmeg	5 mL
1 lb.	phyllo pastry	454 g
1 cup	melted butter or margarine	250 mL

In a bowl, combine feta, cottage cheese, eggs, parsley, and nutmeg. Mix well and set aside.

TO PREPARE THE PHYLLO TRIANGLES: Thaw frozen phyllo in the refrigerator for 24 hours before use. Remove phyllo from the package, unroll, and lay it flat on the counter. Cover with a slightly dampened tea towel. Remove 1 sheet of phyllo and cut into 4 equal-sized strips. Take 2 of the strips, cover the other 2 temporarily, brush with melted butter, and place on top of each other. Place 1 tsp. (5 mL) of food mixture at the bottom end, as shown in figure 2, page 24. Lift the corner of the phyllo so that it forms a right triangle. Continue to fold until a triangle-shaped pita is created. Repeat procedure until required number of triangles are formed. Brush each triangle, top and bottom, with butter and set on a baking sheet, seam-side down. It is not necessary to grease the baking sheet. With the tip of a sharp knife pierce each pita 2 or 3 times to allow steam to escape during baking. Sprinkle with a few drops of water to prevent curling of top layers and encourage even browning. Bake in a preheated 350°F (180°C) oven for 20 minutes or until golden brown.

ADD TO THE GUSTO! Invent your own variations of this recipe. Here's a sample: TO MAKE ONION-DILL PITA: Substitute ½ cup (125 mL) chopped, fresh dill and 2 tbsp. (30 mL) chopped green onions for parsley and nutmeg in the above recipe.

CHEESE ROLLS

Bourekakia Tiri

Method: Roll-up

MAKES ABOUT 40 ROLL-UPS

These delectable entrées are great as appetizers or as a main course. The roll-ups feature a savory Greek cheese filling.

1 tbsp.	olive oil	15 mL
1	red or yellow bell pepper, finely chopped	1
6	green onions, finely chopped	6
2 tbsp.	butter or margarine	30 mL
3 tbsp.	flour	45 mL
1 cup	hot milk	250 mL
2	eggs, lightly beaten	2
2 cups	grated graviera or crumbled feta	500 mL
½ cup	chopped, fresh parsley	125 mL
	freshly ground pepper	
1 lb.	phyllo pastry	454 g
1 cup	melted butter or margarine	250 mL

Heat a skillet over medium-high heat. Add olive oil, bell pepper and green onions. Sauté for a few minutes. Set aside. In a saucepan, melt butter or margarine over medium-low heat. Add flour, stir and blend with a wire whisk. Slowly add hot milk, continuing to stir with the whisk until the mixture thickens. Lower heat and cook for about 3 minutes. Remove from heat and allow to cool slightly. Stir in eggs, cheese, parsley, freshly ground pepper and sautéed mixture. Mix well and set aside. The filling may be prepared 3 days in advance and refrigerated, covered. Assemble phyllo rolls as directed on page 25. Bake in a preheated 350°F (180°C) oven for 20 minutes or until golden brown. Serve warm.

See photograph page 33.

SEAFOOD PITA I

Psaropita I
Method: Triangles
MAKES ABOUT 36 TRIANGLES

Poseidon nods in approval. These flavorful morsels will win the hearts of all seafood lovers.

1 lb.	crab-flavored seafood	454 g
1 cup	chopped green bell pepper	250 mL
10	green onions, finely chopped	10
3 tbsp.	chopped pimientos	45 mL
1 tbsp.	lemon juice	15 mL
1 tsp.	paprika	5 mL
	salt and pepper	
1 cup	Yogurt-Onion Sauce, recipe follows	250 mL
1 lb.	phyllo pastry	454 g
1 cup	melted butter or margarine	250 mL

Chop seafood into bite-size pieces and place in a bowl along with bell pepper, green onions, pimientos, lemon juice, paprika, salt, pepper and *Yogurt-Onion Sauce*. Mix thoroughly and proceed with directions for making *Triangle Pites,* page 24. Bake in a preheated 350°F (180°C) oven for 20 minutes or until golden. Allow to cool 15 minutes before serving.

TO MAKE YOGURT-ONION SAUCE:

6	green onions, chopped	6
2	garlic cloves, minced	2
2 tbsp.	butter or margarine	30 mL
3 tbsp.	flour	45 mL
1½ cups	low-fat yogurt	375 mL

In a skillet, sauté the onions and garlic lightly in butter over medium-low heat. Reduce heat to low and stir in flour with a wire whisk. Add yogurt, stirring constantly until thickened. Cool and use in the recipe above. The cooled sauce may be thinned by stirring in more yogurt. Makes about 1¼ cups (300 mL).

SEAFOOD PITA II

Psaropita II
Method: Triangles
MAKES ABOUT 36 TRIANGLES

Another treat from Poseidon's grotto. These phyllo-wrapped morsels are made with scallops and yogurt sauce.

1 lb.	raw scallops	454 g
	flour for dredging scallops	
2 tbsp.	olive oil	30 mL
4	garlic cloves, minced	4
⅔ cup	chopped, fresh parsley	150 mL
⅔ cup	grated graviera cheese	150 mL
½ cup	Yogurt-Onion Sauce, page 37	125 mL
1 lb.	phyllo pastry	454 g
1 cup	melted butter or margarine	250 mL

Wash and dry the scallops. Dredge with flour. Heat skillet over medium-high heat. Add olive oil, scallops and minced garlic. Sauté quickly for about 3 minutes or until scallops are opaque. Add parsley at the last minute. Transfer to a bowl and allow to cool. Add cheese and *Yogurt-Onion Sauce* and mix well. Place a spoonful of filling on each phyllo strip to make pita triangles as directed on page 24. Bake in a preheated 350°F (180°C) oven for 20 minutes or until golden brown. Cool slightly and serve warm.

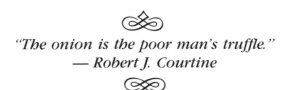

"The onion is the poor man's truffle."
— Robert J. Courtine

CHICKEN PITA

Kotopita

Method: Triangles

MAKES ABOUT 40 TRIANGLES

You'll love this wonderful combination of fresh dill and chicken. Here's a great entrée for brunch or a light lunch.

2 cups	cooked, diced chicken breasts, see method	500 mL
2 tsp.	lemon juice	10 mL
1 cup	Yogurt-Onion Sauce, page 37	250 mL
5	green onions, finely chopped	5
¼ cup	chopped dillweed or 1 tsp. (5 mL) crushed, dry dillweed	50 mL
	salt and pepper	
1 lb.	phyllo pastry	454 g
1 cup	melted butter or margarine	250 mL

Prepare chicken. This may be done in advance. Place skinned, washed chicken breasts in a shallow pan. Cover with aluminum foil and bake in a preheated 350°F (180°C) oven for 45 minutes or until tender but not dry. Do not add liquid. The chicken will cook in its own juices. Cool, bone and dice. Sprinkle lemon juice over chicken and set aside. Combine diced chicken , Yogurt-Onion Sauce, green onions, dillweed, salt and pepper in a bowl. Mix well and proceed with directions for making triangle pitas, page 24. Bake in a preheated oven at 350°F (180°C) for 20 minutes or until golden brown. Cool slightly and serve.

See photograph page 33.

MEAT ROLLS

Bourekakia Kreas
Method: Roll-Up
MAKES ABOUT 40 ROLL-UPS

What a delicious appetizer or side dish! These meat-filled roll-ups have a delightful flavor, enhanced by the special combination of herbs and spices.

2 tbsp.	olive oil	30 mL
1 lb.	lean ground beef, pork or lamb	500 g
1	medium onion, finely chopped	1
2	garlic cloves, minced or crushed through a press	2
¼ cup	chopped, fresh parsley	50 mL
2 tbsp.	tomato paste	30 mL
½ cup	water	125 mL
½ cup	white wine	125 mL
¼ tsp.	sugar	1 mL
½ tsp.	cinnamon	2 mL
½ tsp.	grated nutmeg	2 mL
½ tsp.	crushed, dry oregano	2 mL
	salt and pepper	
½ cup	grated Parmesan or kefalotiri cheese	125 mL
¼ cup	bread crumbs	50 mL
1 lb.	phyllo pastry	454 g
1 cup	melted butter or margarine	250 mL

Heat a skillet over medium-high heat, add olive oil and sauté meat until brown. Add onion and garlic. Continue to cook until the onion is soft and translucent. Stir in the parsley, tomato paste, water, wine, sugar, cinnamon, nutmeg, oregano, salt and pepper. Simmer for 40 minutes or until the liquid is absorbed. Remove from heat, stir in cheese and bread crumbs. Allow to cool. Proceed with directions for making pita roll-ups as described on page 25. Bake in a preheated oven at 350°F (180°C) oven for 20 minutes or until golden brown. Cool slightly and serve.

PASTITSIO PITA

Pastitsio Pita
Method: In-The-Pan
MAKES 12-14 SERVINGS

Here's a new touch. The perennial casserole favorite — _Pastitsio_ — is layered in phyllo pastry to create a dazzling and appetizing entrée.

	Meat Sauce, Macaroni and Thin Egg Sauce, page 76	
1 lb.	phyllo pastry	454 g
1 cup	melted butter or margarine	250 mL

Prepare the Meat Sauce, Macaroni, and Thin Egg Sauce as described in the Pastitsio recipe on page 76. Butter a rectangular pan measuring approximately 9" x 12" x 2 ½" (23 cm x 30 cm x 6.5 cm). Lay a phyllo sheet on the bottom of the pan and brush with butter. Layer 7 additional sheets of phyllo, buttering each as you go. Spread half the Macaroni evenly over the phyllo and pour half the Thin Egg Sauce over it. Next, spread all the Meat Sauce over the Macaroni. Cover the Meat layer with remaining Macaroni and pour remaining Thin Egg Sauce over it. Shake the pan gently to allow the sauce to penetrate. Top with 8 additional phyllo sheets, again buttering each as you go. Finish by buttering the top sheet. With a sharp knife, cut through the top 4 layers of the phyllo. This will make cutting and serving after baking easier. Bake in a preheated 350°F (180°C) oven for 45 minutes or until golden. Remove from oven, allow to cool for 10 minutes, cut through, and serve.

"When it comes to food," remarked comic writer James Thurber, "Looks can be deceiving ... it's eating that's believing!"

The chef's hat is said to be of Greek origin, being a white version of the Greek monk's hat. In olden days, famous cooks took refuge in monasteries to avoid persecution by foreign invaders.

VEGETABLES
Lahanika

A good cook will tell you that the art of cooking begins in the garden. Fresh vegetables provide tastier meals and, from a nutritional point of view, contribute to a balanced diet by providing necessary fiber, carbohydrates, vitamins and minerals. Use garden-fresh vegetables whenever possible. Avoid overcooking them to preserve maximum flavor and nutritional benefits. The rich colors and textures of vegetables add much to visual pleasure in a well-prepared meal which in turn heightens the appetite.

VEGETABLE CASSEROLE

Briami

MAKES 6 SERVINGS

This meal reaches its zenith when it's prepared with garden fresh vegetables. Garlic and fennel provide the distinctive flavor. A light and nutritious feast.

½ cup	chicken stock, page 141	125 mL
2 tbsp.	olive oil	30 mL
2	garlic cloves, crushed through a press or minced	2
½ tsp	crushed fennel seed	2 mL
¼ tsp.	sugar	1 mL
	salt and pepper	
	olive oil to grease casserole	
1	small onion, sliced	1
4	large carrots, cut in ¼" (5mm) slices	4
4	large parsnips, cut in ¼ (5mm) slices	4
3	large tomatoes, blanched, peeled, seeded and chopped or 14 oz. (398 mL) can tomatoes drained and chopped	3
½ cup	chopped, fresh parsley	125 mL

Combine chicken stock, olive oil, garlic, fennel seed, sugar, salt and pepper in a bowl. Stir well and set aside. Grease a 6-cup (1.5 L) ovenproof casserole lightly with olive oil. Arrange a layer of onion slices on the bottom and top with a layer each of carrots and parsnips. Cover with a layer of tomato and sprinkling of parsley. Pour some of the chicken stock mixture over the vegetables. Repeat the process until all the ingredients have been used. Cover casserole with a lid or aluminum foil and bake in a preheated 350°F (180°C) oven for 1 hour or until vegetables are tender. Remove lid for the last 15 minutes of baking. Sprinkle with fresh parsley just before serving.

NOTE: As a variation, add or substitute zucchini, eggplant or celery. Fresh or dry dillweed, used instead of fennel, provides another special flavor.

OKRA AND TOMATOES

Bamies me Domates
MAKES 4-6 SERVINGS

This delightful vegetarian dish consists of tender green morsels of okra, smothered in onions and tomato sauce. Serve it as a first course, or as a complete meal with crusty bread, feta and a robust Greek wine.

1 lb.	fresh okra or 2 x 10 oz. (284 g) packages, frozen	500 g
2 tbsp.	olive oil	30 mL
1	large onion, finely chopped	1
3	garlic cloves, minced	3
2 cups	chopped tomatoes, blanched and peeled	500 mL
¼ cup	chopped, fresh parsley	50 mL
½ tsp.	sugar	2 mL
1	lemon, juice of	1
¾ cup	water or wine	175 mL
	salt and pepper	
	parsley sprigs for garnish	

Wash okra and pat dry. Cut off stems, taking care not to expose the seeds in the pods. Set aside. Heat a sauté pan over medium-high heat, add olive oil, onion and garlic. Sauté until lightly browned and soft. Stir in okra, chopped tomatoes, parsley, sugar, lemon juice, water or wine, salt and pepper. Bring to a boil, cover and reduce heat to medium-low. Simmer for 30 minutes or until okra is tender. Place in a serving dish and garnish with parsley.

GREEN BEANS AND FETA

Fassolakia Feta

MAKES 6-8 SERVINGS

Sheer ambrosia! Garden-fresh green beans and feta — accented with dillweed — make an irresistible combination. This baked casserole may be served either warm or cold.

2 lbs.	fresh green beans	1 kg
4 tbsp.	olive oil	60 mL
1	large onion, finely chopped	1
3	garlic cloves, minced or crushed through a press	3
½ cup	chopped, fresh parsley	125 mL
1 tbsp.	chopped dillweed or ½ tsp. (2 mL) crushed, dry dillweed	15 mL
¾ cup	water	175 mL
	freshly ground pepper	
1 cup	crumbled feta	250 mL

Wash, trim and snap beans into 2" (5 cm) lengths. Heat a sauté pan over medium-high heat. Add olive oil, onion and garlic. Sauté until onion is transparent. Stir in parsley and dillweed. Toss beans with onion mixture and transfer to a shallow casserole measuring approximately 8" x 12" x 2" (20 cm x 30 cm x 5 cm). Add water, cover with aluminum foil and bake in a preheated 375°F (190°C) oven for 45 minutes or until tender and liquid has been absorbed. Remove from oven, cool slightly, and transfer to a large bowl. Grind pepper over the beans and toss with feta. Serve with baked new potatoes and fish or meat.

For a healthy life and longevity, Plato advised his disciples to eat lots of legumes.

BRAISED CAULIFLOWER

Kounoupithi me Saltsa
MAKES 6-8 SERVINGS

Sautéed onion and garlic, accented with tomato and lemon, develop a zesty sauce in this steamed cauliflower dish.

1	large cauliflower	1
3 tbsp.	olive oil	45 mL
1	medium onion, finely chopped	1
3	garlic cloves, minced	3
1 tbsp.	tomato paste	15 mL
1 cup	water	250 mL
1	lemon, juice of	1
¼ tsp.	sugar	1 mL
	salt and pepper	

Wash the cauliflower and separate into florets. Place a vegetable steamer in a saucepan and add enough water to just cover the bottom of the steamer. Bring to a boil, add cauliflower and steam over high heat for 4 minutes. Set aside. Meanwhile, heat a sauté pan over medium-high heat and add olive oil, onion and garlic. Sauté until onion is transparent. Mix tomato paste with water and stir into the onion, along with lemon juice, sugar, salt and pepper. Bring the mixture to a boil, lower heat and simmer for about 3 minutes. Transfer cauliflower to the tomato sauce. Bring to a quick boil, reduce to a simmer, cover, and cook, with lid slightly askew, until cauliflower is tender.

NOTES: Another popular Greek way of serving steamed cauliflower is with EGG-LEMON SAUCE, page 137, or LEMON-OIL DRESSING, page 138, omitting the tomato sauce.

❧

"One is rich, not through possessions, but through that which one can with dignity do without."
— *Epicurus*

❧

EGGPLANT CUSTARD

Melitzanogalaktopita

MAKES 4-6 SERVINGS

Rather than milk, this piquant baked custard is made with yogurt. The delicate flavor of the eggplant blends in beautifully to produce a delightful entrée.

2	medium eggplants	2
3 tbsp.	olive oil	45 mL
1	small onion, finely chopped	1
⅓ cup	chopped, fresh parsley	75 mL
¼ tsp.	chopped dillweed or⅛ tsp. (0.5 mL) crushed, dry dillweed	1 mL
2	eggs	2
2	egg whites	2
1 cup	thick, rich yogurt	250 mL
1 tsp.	lemon juice	5 mL
	salt and pepper	

Halve the eggplants and brush lightly with 1 tbsp. (15 mL) olive oil. Place, cut-side down, on a baking sheet and bake in a 350°F (180°C) oven for 45 minutes or until soft. Remove from oven and allow to cool. Scoop pulp into a bowl, beat with electric beater until smooth. Set aside. Heat remaining oil in a skillet and sauté onion until translucent. Stir in parsley and dillweed. Cool slightly. In a separate bowl, beat eggs and egg whites until fluffy. Stir in yogurt, lemon juice, salt, pepper and sautéed onion mixture. Pour into a greased shallow casserole measuring approximately 6" x 10" x 2" (15 cm x 25 cm x 5 cm). Set inside a larger baking pan and add enough boiling water between the 2 pans to come half-way up the casserole. Bake in a preheated 325°F (160°C) oven for 1 hour or until a knife inserted in the custard comes out clean. Allow to cool for 10 minutes before serving.

ZUCCHINI WITH FETA

Kolokithakia Feta
MAKES 8-10 SERVINGS

Feta cheese has a distinctive flavor and a delightful affinity for zucchini and tomato. A truly ethnic and delicious Greek dish.

6	**medium zucchini**	6
½ cup	**olive oil**	125 mL
1	**medium onion, thinly sliced**	1
6	**tomatoes, sliced or 19 oz. (540 mL) can tomatoes, drained and chopped**	6
1½ cups	**crumbled feta**	375 mL
¾ cup	**chopped, fresh parsley**	175 mL
¼ cup	**water or white wine**	50 mL
	salt and pepper	
1 tbsp.	**butter (optional)**	15 mL

Preheat broiler. Wash zucchini, pat dry and slice lengthwise into slices about ¼" (5 mm) thick. Brush both sides lightly with olive oil, arrange on baking sheet and broil until golden. Set aside. Lightly oil a casserole which measures about 8" x 12" x 2" (20 cm x 30 cm x 5 cm). Alternately layer zucchini, onion slices, tomato, feta, parsley, salt and pepper, ending with zucchini. Top with crumbled feta. Add water or wine, dot with butter and bake, uncovered, in a preheated 375°F (190°C) oven for 30 minutes or until ingredients are bubbling and the topping is lightly browned.

"LITTLE SHOES"

Papoutsakia
MAKES 12 SERVINGS

Don't you love that name? The vegetables — zucchini or small eggplants — do look like funny little shoes when they're halved and stuffed with vegetables and cheese.

6	zucchini or small eggplants	6
¼ cup	olive oil	50 mL
1	small onion, finely chopped	1
2	garlic cloves, minced	2
⅓ cup	long-grain rice	75 mL
½ cup	tomato sauce	125 mL
½ cup	water	125 mL
¼ cup	chopped, fresh parsley	50 mL
1 tsp.	crushed, dry mint	5 mL
	salt and pepper	
	grated Parmesan cheese	
1 cup	water (for baking pan)	250 mL

Wash zucchini (or eggplant) and cut in half lengthways. Scoop out pulp from the centers with a melon scoop. Chop pulp and reserve, along with the shells. In a skillet, heat oil and sauté the onion and garlic until the onion is tender. Add the vegetable pulp and continue to sauté for 5 minutes. Add rice, tomato sauce mixed with water, parsley, mint, salt and pepper. Cook for 20 minutes or until liquid is absorbed.

Place zucchini or eggplant in a baking dish. Fill shells with the cooked mixture. Top with grated cheese. Pour 1 cup (250 mL) of water into the baking pan. Cover with aluminum foil and bake in a preheated 350°F (180°C) oven for 45 minutes. Remove foil and bake for an additional 10 minutes.

ADD TO THE GUSTO! For a richer version, sauté onion with ½ lb. lean ground beef (250 g) and proceed as above.

See photograph opposite.

VEGETABLES —

BAKED EGGPLANT

Imam Baildi

MAKES 6 SERVINGS

IMAM BAILDI is a baked casserole made by stuffing eggplant with garlic, tomatoes and fresh herbs. Legend has it that "A priest (*Imam*) swooned in ecstasy when he took the first bite" — hence its unusual name.

3	medium eggplants	3
	salt	
6 tbsp.	olive oil	90 mL
1	medium onion, finely chopped	1
4	garlic cloves, minced	4
14 oz.	can of tomato sauce	398 mL
½ cup	chopped, fresh parsley	125 mL
2 tbsp.	chopped mint or 1 tsp. (5 mL) crushed, dry mint	30 mL
½ cup	currants	125 mL
	salt and pepper	
¼ cup	water or wine	50 mL
	olive oil for drizzling	
	parsley sprigs for garnish	

Wash eggplants, dry, remove stems and cut in half lengthwise. With a knife, make 4 deep channels on the flat sides of the eggplants, careful not to cut through the purple skin. Sprinkle with salt and let stand in a colander for 30 minutes. Meanwhile, prepare the filling.

TO PREPARE FILLING: Heat a sauté pan over medium-high heat, add 2 tbsp. (30 mL) olive oil, onion and garlic. Sauté until onion is transparent. Stir in tomato sauce, half the parsley, mint, currants, salt, pepper and water or wine. Simmer for 30 minutes. Cool slightly.

Rinse the eggplant halves with cold water, drain and pat dry. Brush surfaces with remaining olive oil and place on a baking sheet. Broil until browned.

Stuff the channels of the eggplants with the filling. Allow a small amount to cover tops. Sprinkle with remaining parsley, drizzle with olive oil. Cover with aluminum foil, bake in a preheated 350°F (180°C) oven for 1 hour or until eggplant is tender. Garnish with sprigs of parsley.

EGGPLANT AND FETA

Melitzanes me Feta Fournou
MAKES ABOUT 12 SERVINGS

Here's another meal-in-itself casserole. Once you've tried this, it's bound to become a regular.

2	medium eggplants	2
¼ cup	olive oil	50 mL
1	large onion, finely chopped	1
3	garlic cloves, minced	3
2	celery ribs, minced	2
19 oz.	can tomatoes, chopped, with juice	540 mL
2	bay leaves	2
¼ tsp.	sugar	1 mL
½ tsp.	crushed, dry basil	2 mL
½ tsp.	crushed, dry savory	2 mL
	freshly ground pepper	
8 oz.	mozzarella cheese, sliced	227 g
16 oz.	2% cottage cheese	500 g
1 cup	crumbled feta	250 mL
¼ cup	bread crumbs	50 mL

Wash the eggplant, cut off the green stem and peel, allowing some peel to remain in alternate strips. Cut into ½" (1 cm) slices. Salt both sides and stack between sheets of paper toweling. Place a plate or other weight on top and allow to sit for 30 minutes. Meanwhile, heat a sauté pan over medium-high heat. Add 2 tbsp. (30 mL) of olive oil, onion, garlic and celery. Sauté until onion is translucent. Stir in tomatoes with juice, bay leaves, sugar, basil, savory and pepper. Simmer for 35 minutes or until most of the liquid has been absorbed. Remove from heat, cool slightly and discard bay leaves. Brush both sides of the eggplant with olive oil, place on a cookie sheet and broil on both sides until golden. Set aside. Lightly oil a casserole measuring approximately 9" x 13" x 2" (23 cm x 33 cm x 5 cm). Sprinkle with bread crumbs, place half the eggplant in a single layer over crumbs. Lay down mozzarella slices, then half the tomato sauce mixture. Follow with all of the cottage cheese. Top with a final layer of eggplant, crumbled feta and the remaining tomato sauce. Bake in a preheated 350°F (180°C) oven for 45 minutes or until golden. Cool for 10 minutes before serving. Serve with crusty bread and a robust Greek wine.

GREEK POTATO SALAD

Patatosalata
MAKES 6-8 SERVINGS

For optimum flavor, prepare the dressing an hour in advance and allow to stand at room temperature. This potato salad is served warm.

DRESSING

4 parts	olive oil	4 parts
1 part	wine vinegar or lemon juice	1 part
1	garlic clove, mashed	1
	oregano, fresh or crushed, dry	
	pinch of sugar	
	salt and freshly ground pepper	
2 lbs.	red waxy potatoes	1 kg
10	green onions, chopped	10
	fresh parsley, chopped, for garnish	

To prepare the dressing, combine and whisk olive oil, vinegar or lemon juice, garlic, oregano, sugar, salt and pepper in a bowl. Transfer to a jar, cover with a lid and allow to sit at room temperature for at least 1 hour.

Wash the potatoes and place in a large saucepan. Cover with water. Bring to a boil, reduce heat and simmer, covered, until fork-tender, about 30-45 minutes. Remove with a slotted spoon and cool just enough to handle. Peel while still warm and cut into thick wedges or cubes. Place in a warm bowl. Toss gently with the dressing and green onions. Garnish with parsley and serve warm.

"Let the sky rain potatoes."
— Shakespeare. The Merry Wives of Windsor

BAKED OMELETTE

Omeletta Fournou

MAKES 4-6 SERVINGS

Served with sliced feta and vine-ripened tomatoes, this omelette provides a satisfying light meal in itself.

2 tbsp.	olive oil	30 mL
2	medium zucchini, diced or 5 small zucchini, sliced	2/5
16	green onions, finely chopped	16
12	eggs, lightly beaten	12
¼ cup	milk	50 mL
1 tbsp.	chopped dillweed or ½ tsp. (2 mL) crushed, dry dillweed	15 mL
	salt and pepper	

Heat a skillet over medium-high heat. Add olive oil, zucchini and onions. Sauté until lightly browned. Cool. Beat the eggs and milk until light and fluffy. Stir the cooled zucchini, dillweed, salt and pepper into the egg mixture. Lightly oil a shallow medium-size casserole and pour the zucchini mixture into it, allowing ¾" (15mm) of space at the top. Bake in a preheated 375°F (190°C) oven for 35 minutes or until the omelette is puffed, golden and firm. A knife inserted in the omelette should come out clean.

ADD TO THE GUSTO! TO MAKE BAKED SEAFOOD OMELETTE: Sauté green onions lightly in butter. Add crab meat or shrimp and chopped parsley. Heat through. Cool slightly. Stir into egg mixture and proceed as above.

TO MAKE BAKED TOMATO OMELETTE: Blanch 6 medium tomatoes, peel, halve, seed and cut in strips. Substitute tomatoes for zucchini and oregano for dillweed in the above recipe. Proceed as directed.

SPINACH SOUFFLÉ

Spanaki Soufflé
MAKES 2 SERVINGS

This light meal is easy to make and wonderfully satisfying. It will serve 4 as a side dish or 2 as a meal. After making it once, try the variations at the bottom of the page.

3 tbsp.	butter or margarine	45 mL
4 tbsp.	flour	60 mL
1 cup	hot skim milk	250 mL
4	egg yolks, lightly beaten	4
6	green onions, finely chopped	6
1	bunch fresh spinach, cooked, squeezed dry and chopped	1
½ cup	crumbled feta	125 mL
	freshly ground pepper	
6	egg whites	6

Melt butter or margarine in a saucepan over low heat. Add flour, mix well. Add hot milk, stirring constantly with a wire whisk. Cook over low heat for 1-2 minutes, cool slightly, then stir in beaten yolks, onions, spinach, feta and pepper. Blend well and set aside to cool. Beat the egg whites until they hold a stiff peak, do not overbeat. Stir 2 tbsp. (30 mL) of the beaten whites into the egg yolk-spinach mixture. Gently fold in the remaining whites with a spatula. Pour into a lightly buttered, high-sided casserole or soufflé dish. Bake in a preheated 375°F (190°C) oven for 45 to 50 minutes or until the soufflé rises fully and is golden brown. Serve immediately.

NOTES: A 10-oz. (283 g) package of frozen chopped spinach may be subsituted for fresh spinach. Fresh tomatoes and Kalamata olives make an excellent accompaniment for this dish.

VARIATION: SPANAKORIZO SOUFFLÉ: Use the above recipe, but make the following changes: Add ¾ cup (175 mL) SPINACH RICE PILAF (*Spanakorizo*) see page 59, ½ tsp. (2 mL) paprika and ½ tsp. (2 mL) salt. Omit the feta and black pepper.

STUFFED TOMATOES

Yemista

MAKES 5-6 SERVINGS

Whether vegetarian or not, you'll adore these rice-stuffed tomatoes. This popular Greek dish is an excellent keeper; in fact, the flavor is enhanced the day after it's made.

10	large tomatoes	10
3 tbsp.	olive oil	45 mL
1	medium onion, finely chopped	1
4	garlic cloves, minced	4
1 cup	raw long-grain rice	250 mL
1 cup	hot water	250 mL
½ cup	chopped, fresh parsley	125 mL
3 tbsp.	chopped dillweed, or 1½ tsp. (7 mL) crushed, dry dillweed	45 mL
	salt and pepper	
	sugar	
	olive oil for basting	
	water for pan	

Wash and dry the tomatoes, cut off about ½" (1 cm) from the tops. Scoop out the pulp and juice, allowing thick shells to remain. Chop pulp and reserve with juice. Arrange the hollowed-out tomatoes in a lightly oiled shallow casserole and set aside. Heat a sauté pan over medium-high heat, add olive oil, onion and garlic. Sauté for a few minutes until onion is translucent. Stir in rice, hot water, parsley, dillweed, salt, pepper and the reserved chopped pulp and juice. Simmer, uncovered, over medium-low heat until the liquid is just absorbed. Allow to cool slightly. Sprinkle a pinch of sugar into each tomato. Stuff tomatoes about two-thirds full with the mixture. Stuff loosely to allow for expansion of the rice as it cooks. Replace tops and brush tomatoes with olive oil. Add enough water to just cover the bottom of the casserole pan. Bake in a preheated 350°F (180°C) oven for 60 minutes. Allow to cool slightly before serving.

NOTES: TO PREPARE STUFFED BELL PEPPERS: Add 2 cups (500 mL) fresh or canned chopped tomatoes to the mixture. To vary the stuffing, add 3 tbsp. (45 mL) currants, raisins, and/or toasted pine nuts.

See photograph page 51.

SPINACH RICE PILAF

Spanakorizo
MAKES 4 SERVINGS

This Greek classic is a crowd pleaser. It's a splendid side dish or main course. Accompanied with wedges of juicy-ripe tomatoes, Kalamata olives, toasted pine nuts and slices of feta, it's simply delicious! Serve hot or cold.

2	bunches fresh spinach	2
2 tbsp.	olive oil	30 mL
1	large onion, finely chopped	1
1 cup	converted long-grain rice	250 mL
1½ cups	water	375 mL
1 tbsp.	chopped dillweed or ½ tsp. (2 mL) crushed, dry dillweed	15 mL
	salt and pepper	
	lemon wedges for garnish	

Wash spinach thoroughly and drain well. Tear larger leaves into smaller pieces. Set aside. Heat a large sauté pan over medium-high heat, add olive oil and onions. Sauté until onion is transparent. Add rice, continue sautéing for an additional 2 to 3 minutes. Stir in water, dillweed, salt and pepper. Bring to a boil, add spinach and stir to combine ingredients. Bring to a boil for the second time, cover and cook on low setting for 30 minutes, or until liquid is completely absorbed. Allow to cool slightly. Serve warm, garnished with lemon wedges.

NOTES: For a tomato accent, add 2 to 4 tbsp. (30 to 60 mL) of tomato paste. This recipe may also be varied by substituting mint, oregano or parsley for the dillweed.

EGGPLANT PILAF

Pilafi Melitzanes

MAKES 8 SERVINGS

The eggplant — that wonderful, oversized, smooth-skinned berry — has long been prized by the Greeks for its delicate, melt-in-your-mouth flavor and kitchen versatility.

1	medium eggplant	1
2	medium zucchini	2
¼ cup	olive oil	50 mL
1	medium onion, finely chopped	1
4	garlic cloves, minced	4
½ cup	chopped, fresh parsley	125 mL
1 tsp.	crushed, dry oregano	5 mL
½ tsp.	crushed, dry thyme	2 mL
2	bay leaves	2
28 oz.	can tomatoes, drained, chopped	796 mL
	salt and pepper	
1 cup	raw long-grain rice	250 mL
3 cups	chicken stock, page 141	750 mL
½ cup	white wine	125 mL
½ cup	crumbled feta	125 mL
1 tbsp.	butter or margarine	15 mL

Wash eggplant, dry and cut, unpeeled, into ¾" (2 cm) slices. Cut crossways to make ¾" cubes. Salt the cubes, place in a bowl lined with paper toweling, weigh down with a plate, and let stand for 30 minutes. Cut zucchini into ½" (1 cm) slices and set aside. Heat a sauté pan over medium-high heat, add olive oil, eggplant and zucchini. Sauté, turning frequently until lightly browned. Reduce heat slightly, add onion and garlic. Continue to sauté until onion is transparent. Stir in parsley, oregano, thyme, bay leaves, tomatoes, salt and pepper. Simmer for 10 minutes or until most of the liquid is absorbed. Transfer the vegetables to a shallow casserole 9" x 13" x 2" (23 cm x 33 cm x 5 cm). Add rice, hot chicken stock, wine and mix well. Sprinkle cheese over casserole, dot with butter, and bake, uncovered, in a preheated 400°F (200°C) oven for 30 minutes or until the liquid is absorbed.

NOTES: Parmesan may be substituted for the feta. As a variation, add cooked shrimp to leftover baked casserole and transform it into a delicious seafood entrée.

ARTICHOKE PILAF

Pilafi Anginares

MAKES 6 SERVINGS

One of our favorite ways to prepare artichokes is in a pilaf such as this. Here's a basic Greek dish that's quick and easy to prepare with frozen artichokes and tastes great. Serve it with wedges of feta.

9 oz.	package frozen artichokes	255 g
1	lemon, juice of	1
2 tbsp.	olive oil	30 mL
1	medium onion, finely chopped	1
1 cup	long-grain rice	250 mL
2 cups	chicken stock, page 141	500 mL
2 tbsp.	tomato paste	30 mL
¼ cup	chopped dillweed or 2 tsp. (10 mL) crushed, dry dillweed	50 mL
	salt and pepper	

Thaw frozen artichokes, sprinkle with lemon juice and set aside. Heat a sauté pan over medium-high heat. Add olive oil and onion. Sauté until onion is tender. Add rice and continue to sauté for 3 minutes, stirring constantly. Add artichokes. In a saucepan, combine chicken stock, tomato paste, dillweed, salt and pepper. Bring to a boil. Pour the stock over the rice and artichokes. Stir gently. Cover and simmer over low heat until the liquid is absorbed, about 25 minutes. Remove from heat and allow to cool slightly before serving.

CINARA, a young and unfortunate beauty, had the ill-luck to displease a vindictive and irascible god who metamorphosed her into the ARTICHOKE.

MEATLESS MOUSSAKA I

Moussakas Horis Kreas I
MAKES ABOUT 12 SERVINGS

This is a lighter version of the traditional meat-filled *Moussaka*. It's a tasty and satisfying one-dish casserole. Serve it with crusty whole-grain bread and a Greek red wine to make a complete meal.

2	medium eggplants	2
2	medium zucchini	2
12	large mushrooms	12
¼ cup	olive oil	50 mL
2 tbsp.	olive oil	30 mL
2	medium onions, finely chopped	2
3	garlic cloves, minced	3
6	tomatoes, blanched, peeled, and chopped or 19 oz. (540 mL) can tomatoes, drained and chopped	6
½ cup	white wine	125 mL
1 tsp.	crushed, dry oregano	5 mL
¼ tsp.	sugar	1 mL
	salt and pepper	
1½ cups	crumbled feta	375 mL

Wash the eggplants and cut off the green stems. Peel the eggplant, allowing some of the peel to remain in alternate strips. Cut into ½" (1 cm) slices. Salt both sides and stack between sheets of paper toweling. Place a plate or other weight on top and allow the eggplant to sit for 30 minutes. Peel zucchini in the same manner and slice lengthwise into ¼" (5 mm) slices. Clean mushrooms and cut in thin slices.

EGGPLANT: To peel or not to peel, that is the question! Some cooks do, others don't. The purplish skin is edible. Peel it if it's tough and fibrous. To salt or not to salt? Again, a debatable point. We salt and drain sliced eggplant because it draws out moisture and bitterness and keeps the eggplant from absorbing as much oil when it's cooked.

MEATLESS MOUSSAKA I

Continued

Brush olive oil on both sides of eggplant, zucchini and mushroom slices. Place on a baking sheet and set under the broiler. Broil until the vegetables are golden brown on both sides. Set aside. Heat a sauté pan over medium-high heat, add 2 tbsp. (30 mL) olive oil, onions and garlic. Sauté until onions are transparent. Stir in tomatoes, wine, oregano, sugar, salt and pepper. Bring to a boil, reduce to a simmer, and cook for 30 minutes. Remove from heat and allow to cool slightly. Lightly oil a rectangular casserole, approximately 9" x 12" x 2 ½" (23 cm x 30 cm x 6.5 cm).

TO ASSEMBLE: Start by placing a layer of eggplant slices side-by-side to cover the bottom of the pan. Next, spread a layer of tomato sauce over the eggplant, then a layer of feta. Follow with a layer of zucchini, mushrooms, more tomato sauce, and another layer of feta. Finish with a final layer of eggplant, feta and tomato sauce. Top with THICK CUSTARD SAUCE, page 136. Place in a preheated 350°F (180°C) oven and bake for 45 minutes or until golden. Allow to cool for 15 minutes before serving.

MEATLESS MOUSSAKA II

Moussakas Horis Kreas II
MAKES 12 SERVINGS

This fresh-tasting custardy casserole features the subtle flavors of zucchini and Greek graviera cheese. A vegetarian's delight.

4 cups	cooked brown rice	1 L
6	large zucchini	6
4 tbsp.	olive oil	60 mL
1	large onion, finely chopped	1
4	garlic cloves, minced	4
19 oz.	can tomatoes, drained	540 mL
⅓ cup	chopped, fresh parsley	75 mL
½ cup	toasted pine nuts	125 mL
1 tsp.	crushed, dry mint	5 mL
	salt and pepper	
¼ cup	bread crumbs	50 mL
1 cup	grated graviera or Parmesan	250 mL
4 cups	Thick Custard Sauce, page 136	1 L

Cook rice according to package directions and reserve. Wash and dry zucchini. Trim ends and peel, allowing some peel to remain in alternate strips. Cut lengthwise into ¼" (5 mm) slices. Brush zucchini slices with olive oil, place on a baking sheet, brown both sides under the broiler and set aside. Heat a skillet over medium-high heat, add 1 tbsp. (15 mL) olive oil, onion and garlic. Sauté until onion is translucent; lower heat, chop and stir in tomatoes, parsley, pine nuts, mint, salt, pepper and cooked rice. Set aside.

TO ASSEMBLE: Grease a 9" x 13" x 2" (23 cm x 33 cm x 5 cm) casserole and sprinkle with bread crumbs. Arrange a layer of zucchini slices over the bread crumbs. Spread half the rice-tomato mixture over it, top with a layer of grated graviera or Parmesan, follow with remaining zucchini slices and the rice-tomato mixture. Top with a layer of THICK CUSTARD SAUCE. Bake in a preheated 350°F (180°C) oven for 45 minutes, or until topping is golden. Cool for 15 minutes before serving.

GREEK PIZZA

Pitsa

MAKES 6-8 SERVINGS

Here's a delicious easy-to-make pizza loaded with healthy ingredients: sweet peppers, olives, feta and anchovies. Curiously, pizza is of Greek origin and this version demonstrates what happens when Greek meets Italian in North America.

6	prepared pizza crusts, 6" (15 cm) or 3 x 12" (30 cm) crusts	6
3 tbsp.	olive oil	45 mL
7 ½ oz.	can tomato sauce	213 mL
½ tsp.	crushed, dry thyme	2 mL
1 tsp.	crushed, dry oregano	5 mL
1	small onion, thinly sliced	1
1	yellow bell pepper, thinly sliced	1
1	green bell pepper, thinly sliced	1
6	green onions, finely sliced	6
12	Kalamata olives, pitted and halved	12
2 x 1¾ oz.	tins anchovy fillets	100 g
1 cup	crumbled feta	250 mL

Preheat oven to 400°F (200°C). Brush each pizza crust, top and bottom, with oil and place on a baking sheet. Coat each with tomato sauce. Sprinkle with crushed thyme and oregano. Heat skillet over medium heat, add remaining olive oil and onion rings. Sauté lightly until translucent, then spread over the tomato sauce. Arrange slices of yellow and green peppers on the pizza and dot with green onions and olives. Distribute anchovy slices over this. Sprinkle the pizzas evenly with feta. Bake in a preheated 400°F (200°C) oven for 20 minutes or until the crust in golden.

ADD TO THE GUSTO! Improve the flavor by using homemade Greek Tomato Sauce, page 139.

In ancient Greece, the art of cookery was proclaimed the greater of the fine arts because "It is the more consistent bringer of pleasure."

PASTA & GRAINS
Zimarika kai Dimitriaka

James Beard observed that pasta is one of the most popular foods in existence and as versatile as any single food can be. Greeks love pasta — especially macaroni and spaghetti — which they use to make *Pastitsio* and other unique pasta creations. Alternate pasta products which figure in Greek cookery are *Orzo, Hilopites, Trahana* and *Kritharaki. Orzo* (also called *Manestra*) is a tiny, rice-shaped pasta used in soups and pilafs. *Hilopites* are home-made egg noodles, cut into "a thousand pieces". *Trahana* are noodles made of milk or yogurt (The sweet noodles are made of milk, the sour ones of yogurt). *Kritharaki* is a tiny pasta shaped like orzo but larger in size and firmer in texture. Among the grains, rice is the perennial Greek favorite. *Pligouri* (cracked wheat) is also popular and used in many Hellenic recipes.

GREEK SPAGHETTI

Makaronia me Kafto Voutiro
MAKES 4-5 SERVINGS

When less is more! This popular Greek recipe presents a simple, yet delicious way of combining pasta, grated cheese and browned butter sauce.

1 lb.	spaghetti	500 g
½ cup	grated mizithra, kefalotiri or Parmesan	125 mL
½ cup	butter	125 mL

Cook spaghetti according to package directions and drain. Have a large warmed platter ready for use. Sprinkle cheese on the bottom of the platter, then alternately layer spaghetti and cheese, topping with a layer of cheese. While the spaghetti is cooking, prepare the browned butter sauce.

BUTTER SAUCE: Melt butter in a saucepan over medium-high heat, watching it closely and stirring frequently. It will foam, then change color from yellow to brown. Remove browned butter from heat before it burns, pour over the spaghetti and serve immediately.

ADD TO THE GUSTO! Sprinkle ½ teaspoon (2 mL) cinnamon between layers of pasta and cheese. For variation, use any other pasta product.

NOTE: Cook pasta to the *al dente* stage: tender, but slightly firm in the center.

PASTA & GRAINS —

MACARONI AND FETA

Makaronia me Feta
SERVES 4 to 6

Feta provides a nice accent in this flavorsome macaroni casserole. The croutons add a crunchy texture.

¾ lb.	macaroni, cooked and drained	375 g
¼ cup	melted butter or margarine	50 mL
1½ cups	crumbled feta	375 mL
1½ cups	croutons	375 mL
4	eggs, separated	4
2 cups	milk	500 mL

Cook macaroni according to package directions. Drain, toss with melted butter and ½ cup (125 mL) crumbled feta. Set aside. Lightly oil a shallow 9" x 13" x 2" (23 cm x 33 cm x 5 cm) casserole, sprinkle with another ½ cup (125 mL) feta and half the croutons. Spread the macaroni mixture over this and top with remaining croutons. Beat egg whites until stiff. In a separate bowl beat egg yolks lightly. Fold egg yolks into the whites. Stir in milk, pour mixture over macaroni. Sprinkle with remaining feta. Bake in a preheated 350°F (180°C) oven for 45 minutes or until golden brown.

NOTES: TO PREPARE CROUTONS: Cut half a loaf of day-old bread into small bits and toss in a skillet over medium-high heat with 2 tbsp. (30 mL) olive oil and 2 tbsp. (30 mL) butter. Spread on a baking sheet and bake for 30 minutes at 250°F (120°C). Croutons may be stored in a covered container at room temperature for up to 2 weeks.

MACARONI AND SALMON

Makaronia me Solomo

MAKES 6 SERVINGS

Here's an easy-to-prepare pasta and seafood casserole that's tasty and nutritious. It can be made either with salmon or tuna fish.

2 cups	raw macaroni, penne lisce	500 mL
2	celery ribs, finely chopped	2
1	small onion, finely chopped	1
4 tbsp.	butter or margarine	60 mL
4 tbsp.	flour	60 mL
2 cups	hot milk	500 mL
1 tbsp.	chopped, fresh dill or 1 tsp. (5 mL) dillweed	30 mL
1 tsp.	grated lemon zest	5 mL
	freshly ground pepper	
7 ½ oz.	can salmon, flaked	213 g
½ cup	plain yogurt	125 mL
	croutons, page 71	

Cook the macaroni until it is just tender. While the macaroni is cooking, sauté celery and onion in a skillet in butter or margarine over medium-high heat until onion is tender. Remove from heat. Stir in flour. Whisk in hot milk, a little at a time. Return to low heat and cook for 5 minutes, stirring constantly, until sauce thickens. Cool. Stir in dillweed, lemon zest, pepper, salmon and yogurt. Toss with drained macaroni. Spoon macaroni-onion mixture into a greased casserole measuring approximately 9" x 13" x 2" (23 cm x 33 cm x 5 cm). Top with croutons and bake in a preheated 375°F (190°C) oven for 25 minutes or until golden brown.

MAKARONADA

Makaronada
SERVES 4

Makaronada is macaroni à la Grecque. It's served with a spicy meat sauce and topped with lots of grated cheese. A leafy salad and a Greek wine provide a nice complement.

MEAT SAUCE

3 tbsp.	olive oil	45 mL
1	large onion, chopped	1
3	garlic cloves, minced	3
1	green bell pepper, chopped	1
1 lb.	lean ground beef or lamb	500 g
14 oz.	can tomato sauce	398 mL
1 cup	water	250 mL
½ cup	red wine	125 mL
¼ tsp.	sugar	1 mL
½ tsp	cinnamon	2 mL
3	ground cloves	3
1	bay leaf	1
	salt and pepper	
1 lb.	macaroni (penne lisce, rigatoni) or spaghetti	500 g
	grated mizithra, kefalotiri, Romano or Parmesan	

To make meat sauce, heat a skillet over medium-high heat. Add olive oil, onion, garlic and bell pepper. Sauté until onion is translucent. Stir in ground meat and continue sautéing until meat is lightly browned. Add remaining ingredients, stir, bring to a boil, reduce heat and cover. Simmer, with lid partially askew, for 1 hour.

Cook the pasta according to package directions. Drain and arrange on serving plates. Top with meat sauce and liberal amounts of grated cheese.

PASTA AND MEATBALLS

Makaronia me Keftedes
SERVES 6

Zorba attributed his passion for life to a healthy appetite. Here's a dish to satisfy "the Zorba" in each one of us. Three components — meatballs, tomato sauce and pasta — are combined in this zesty and nutritious meal.

TOMATO SAUCE

3 tbsp.	olive oil	45 mL
2	medium onions, finely chopped	2
3	garlic cloves, minced	3
14 oz.	can tomatoes, chopped, with juice	398 mL
2 x 5 ½ oz.	cans tomato paste	2 x 156 mL
2 cups	water	500 mL
1 cup	dry wine	250 mL
1 tsp.	sugar	5 mL
1	bay leaf	1
1½ tsp.	crushed, dry oregano	7 mL
½ tsp.	cinnamon	2 mL
½ tsp.	ground allspice	2 mL
½ tsp.	grated nutmeg	2 mL
	salt and pepper	

MEATBALLS

1 lb.	lean ground beef	500 g
2	eggs, lightly beaten	2
½ cup	bread crumbs	125 mL
⅓ cup	chopped, fresh parsley	75 mL
1 tsp.	crushed, dry oregano	5 mL
½ tsp.	cinnamon	2 mL
½ tsp.	ground allspice	2 mL
½ tsp.	grated nutmeg	2 mL
	salt and pepper	
3 tbsp.	olive oil	45 mL

PASTA AND MEATBALLS

Continued

SPAGHETTI

	water	
1½ lb.	spaghetti	680 g
¼ cup	olive oil or melted butter	50 mL

TO PREPARE TOMATO SAUCE: Heat a skillet over medium-high heat. Add olive oil, onions and garlic. Sauté until onions are translucent. Stir in remaining ingredients, bring to a boil, reduce to a simmer, cover and cook for 30 minutes. While the sauce is simmering, prepare the meatballs.

TO PREPARE MEATBALLS: Combine all ingredients, except olive oil, in bowl and mix well. Form walnut-sized meatballs in the palm of your hands or in a meatball former. Heat olive oil in a skillet over medium-high heat. Add meatballs and fry until browned. Place on paper toweling to drain. Add meatballs to tomato sauce and simmer slowly for 30 minutes.

TO PREPARE SPAGHETTI: Use a pot large enough to hold, without boiling over, water 3 times the amount of the pasta to be cooked. Bring water to a rolling boil, add pasta gradually so as not to disturb the boil. Cook at a rolling boil until desired degree of doneness is achieved. We prefer *al dente*, tender, but slightly firm in the center. Drain pasta in a colander, return to the pot, and toss with olive oil or melted butter.

TO ASSEMBLE: Serve meatballs over pasta with a liberal sprinkling of grated cheese such as kefalotiri, graviera or Parmesan. If you prefer to bake meatballs see page 15.

PASTITSIO

Pastitsio

MAKES 12 SERVINGS

Pastitsio is without a doubt, the most famous Greek pasta casserole. It is an inspired layering of spicy meat sauce, pasta, grated cheese and custard sauce. Treat yourself and your guests to this most enjoyable classic casserole.

MEAT SAUCE:

4 tbsp.	olive oil or butter	60 mL
1	large onion, finely chopped	1
3	garlic cloves, minced	3
1 lb.	lean ground beef	500 g
14 oz.	can tomatoes, drained and chopped	398 mL
5 ½ oz.	can tomato paste	156 mL
½ cup	water	125 mL
½ cup	red wine	125 mL
½ tsp.	sugar	2 mL
½ tsp.	ground cloves	2 mL
¼ tsp.	cinnamon	1 mL
¼ tsp.	grated nutmeg	1 mL
	salt and pepper	

MACARONI:

1 lb.	long, thin, hollow macaroni (such as bucatini or ziti)	500 g
4 tbsp.	butter or margarine, melted	60 mL
1½ cups	grated mizithra or Parmesan	375 mL

THIN EGG SAUCE:

2	eggs	2
1 cup	milk	250 mL

PASTITSIO

Continued

THICK CUSTARD SAUCE:

4	eggs	4
½ cup	flour	125 mL
2 cups	cold milk	500 mL
2 cups	hot milk	500 mL
¼ tsp.	cinnamon	1 mL
½ tsp.	grated nutmeg	2 mL
	salt and pepper	
	bread crumbs for pan	

TO PREPARE MEAT SAUCE: Heat a large skillet over medium-high heat. Add olive oil, onion and garlic. Sauté until onion is tender. Add ground meat and continue to sauté until meat is lightly browned. Stir in tomatoes, tomato paste, water, wine, sugar, cloves, cinnamon, nutmeg, salt and pepper. Simmer, uncovered, for 30 minutes or until most of the liquid has been absorbed. Set aside.

TO PREPARE MACARONI: Cook according to package directions, drain, and rinse with cool water. Toss with melted butter and 1 cup (250 mL) of the grated cheese. Set aside. Reserve the remaining cheese for the final topping.

TO PREPARE THIN EGG SAUCE: Beat eggs, stir in milk, and set aside.

TO PREPARE THICK CUSTARD SAUCE: Beat eggs in a large saucepan. Add flour gradually, beating continuously until smooth. Stir in cold milk. Slowly add the hot milk, stirring constantly. Cook over medium heat, stirring constantly with a wire whisk, for 10-15 minutes or until mixture is thick. Remove from heat, stir in cinnamon, nutmeg, salt and pepper. Set aside.

TO ASSEMBLE: Grease a casserole measuring about 9" x 12" x 2 ½" (23 cm x 30 cm x 6 cm). Sprinkle lightly with bread crumbs. Place half of the macaroni in the casserole, pour half of the thin sauce over it. Spread the meat sauce on top, then cover with the remaining macaroni. Pour the remaining thin sauce over the macaroni. Top with the thick custard sauce and sprinkle with the reserved grated cheese. Bake in a preheated 350°F (180°C) oven for 1 hour or until custard is golden. Allow to cool for 15 minutes before cutting and serving.

LAMB AND ORZO

Arni Youvetsi

MAKES 4 SERVINGS

Y OUVETSI — named for the clay pot it was originally baked in — is virtually a complete meal in itself. A deep oval enamel roaster is an ideal oven pot for preparing this robust and sumptuous entrée.

2 lbs.	lamb shoulder	1 kg
3 tbsp.	olive oil	45 mL
1	large onion, chopped	1
19 oz.	can tomatoes, chopped with juice	540 mL
2 tbsp.	tomato paste	30 mL
2 cups	water	500 mL
¼ tsp.	cinnamon	1 mL
	salt and pepper	
1 cup	uncooked orzo	250 mL
1¼ cups	boiling water	300 mL
1 tbsp.	butter (optional)	15 mL
	grated Parmesan or Romano	

Trim fat from lamb and cut into 1" (2.5 cm) pieces. In a lightly greased roaster, toss lamb with olive oil, onion, tomatoes and juice, tomato paste, water, cinnamon, salt and pepper. Cover tightly and bake in a preheated 375°F (190°C) oven for 1 hour. Add orzo, boiling water and butter. Cover and bake 30 minutes. Lower heat to 350°F (180°C), uncover, and bake an additional 15 minutes. Serve hot, sprinkled with Parmesan or Romano.

PASTITSIO P.D.Q.

Pastitsio
MAKES 8 SERVINGS

Here's a delightful meat and pasta casserole that's low in calories, high in nutrition, and "pretty-darn quick" to make. We may be making "light" of tradition, but considering the benefits, who's to complain?

2 tbsp.	olive oil	30 mL
1	large onion, finely chopped	1
4	garlic cloves, minced	4
2 lbs.	ground turkey	1 kg
28 oz.	can tomatoes, chopped with juice	796 mL
1 cup	water	250 mL
3 tbsp.	tomato paste	45 mL
2 tsp.	crushed, dry oregano or thyme	10 mL
	salt and pepper	
2 cups	uncooked macaroni or penne lisce	500 mL
	grated Parmesan or kefalotiri	

In a sauteuse (sauté pan), heat oil and sauté onion and garlic until onion is translucent. Add ground meat, break up and brown until meat loses its pinkish color. Add tomatoes with juice, water, tomato paste, oregano or thyme, salt and pepper. Remove from heat.

Grease a shallow, ovenproof casserole, approximately 9" x 13" x 2" (23 cm x 33 cm x 5 cm). Spread ⅓ of the meat mixture in the casserole, then ½ the macaroni, another meat layer, remaining macaroni, and a final meat layer. Bake, covered, in a preheated 350°F (180°C) oven for 30 minutes or until pasta is tender. Remove from oven, uncover, top with grated cheese, and place under broiler for a few minutes to brown. Cut in squares and serve with a green salad and crusty bread.

TOMATO RICE PILAF

Rizi Pilafi
MAKES 8 SERVINGS

Either basil or mint provides an excellent complementary flavor in this baked rice and tomato casserole.

2 tbsp.	butter or margarine	30 mL
1	small onion, finely chopped	1
2	garlic cloves, minced	2
2 cups	raw long-grain rice	500 mL
½ cup	chopped, fresh parsley	125 mL
1 tbsp.	chopped basil or mint or ½ tsp. (2 mL) crushed, dry basil or mint	15 mL
¼ tsp.	sugar	1 mL
	salt and pepper	
19 oz.	can tomatoes, chopped with juice	540 mL
2 ½ cups	chicken stock, page 141	625 mL
1 tbsp.	butter or margarine (optional)	15 mL

Heat butter or margarine in a deep skillet over medium-high heat. Sauté onion and garlic until onion is tender. Add rice and stir until grains are coated. Stir in parsley, basil or mint, sugar, salt, pepper, chopped tomatoes, tomato juice and chicken stock. Bring to a boil. Transfer to a greased deep casserole. Cover and bake in a preheated 400°F (200°C) oven for 30 minutes or until liquid is absorbed and rice is tender. Uncover, toss with butter or margarine, and serve.

See photograph page 103.

❧

"There is in every cook's opinion, no savory dish without the onion. But lest your kissing be spoiled, the onion must be thoroughly boiled."
— Anonymous

❧

CABBAGE RICE PILAF

Lahanorizo
MAKES ABOUT 4 SERVINGS

Hippocrates, the great Greek physician, had a particular affection for cabbage. He prescribed it as a sovereign remedy against many afflictions. So remember the Hippocratic oath: Eat cabbage, it's good for you!

3 tbsp.	olive oil	45 mL
1	large onion, chopped	1
1 cup	long-grain rice	250 mL
3 cups	chopped cabbage	750 mL
2 tbsp.	tomato paste	30 mL
2 cups	hot water	500 mL
¼ cup	chopped, fresh parsley	50 mL
	salt and pepper	

In a deep saucepan, heat oil and sauté onions and rice over medium-high heat. When onion is translucent, add cabbage. Continue to sauté and stir until cabbage is slightly wilted. Stir in tomato paste, water, parsley, salt and pepper. Bring to a boil, reduce heat to lowest setting and cook for 25 minutes or until the liquid is absorbed. Serve with lemon wedges.

ADD TO THE GUSTO! For a different flavor, add freshly chopped dill or caraway seeds.

BULGUR PILAF

Pligouri

MAKES 4 TO 5 SERVINGS

Wheat and grain, a bountiful gift from the goddess Demeter, is regarded by Greeks as the unique food which helped them build their great civilization.

2 tbsp.	olive oil	30 mL
1 cup	bulgur (processed cracked wheat) or cracked wheat	250 mL
1	medium onion, finely chopped	1
1½ cups	hot chicken stock, page 141	375 mL
½ cup	chopped, fresh parsley	125 mL
1 tbsp.	chopped thyme or ½ tsp. (2 mL) crushed, dry thyme	15 mL
	salt and pepper	

Heat 1 tbsp. (15 mL) olive oil in a large sauté pan over medium-high heat. Add bulgur or cracked wheat and sauté, stirring constantly, until grains are lightly browned. Transfer to a plate and set aside. To the sauté pan, add remaining olive oil and onion. Sauté until onion is tender. Stir in bulgur, chicken stock, parsley, thyme, salt and pepper. Bring to a boil, reduce heat to lowest setting, cover, and cook for 16 minutes or until the liquid has been absorbed. (Cracked wheat requires at least 30 minutes to cook). Allow to set, covered, for 10 minutes, fluff with a fork, and serve.

NOTE: Serve as an accompaniment for meat, cheese, or vegetables. Double the recipe and use leftover portions in a salad: Toss cold bulgur with tomatoes, bell pepper slices, green onions, pine nuts, oil, vinegar, salt and pepper.

ORZO AND BULGUR

Orzo me Pligouri
MAKES 6-8 SERVINGS

Bulgur and orzo blend beautifully in this pilaf. Serve this as a side dish, alongside a main course of meat, fish or poultry or as a light meal with crusty bread, cheese and wine.

1 cup	orzo	250 mL
4 tbsp.	olive oil	60 mL
1 cup	bulgur (processed cracked wheat)	250 mL
1	medium onion, finely chopped	1
3	garlic cloves, minced	3
1	bell pepper, finely chopped	1
½ cup	chopped, fresh parsley	125 mL
3 cups	hot chicken stock, page 141	750 mL
1 tbsp.	chopped thyme or ½ tsp. (2 mL) crushed, dry thyme	15 mL
	salt and pepper	
2 tbsp.	lemon juice	30 mL

Parboil the orzo in boiling water for 7 minutes. Drain and set aside. Heat 2 tbsp. (30 mL) olive oil in a sauté pan over medium-high heat. Add bulgur and sauté for 5 minutes or until the bulgur is lightly toasted, stirring constantly. Remove bulgur and set aside. Add remaining olive oil, onion, garlic and bell pepper to the pan. Sauté until onion is translucent. Stir the toasted bulgur, parsley, chicken stock, thyme, salt, pepper, lemon juice and orzo into the onion mixture. Bring to a boil, cover, and reduce heat to lowest setting. Cook for 20 minutes or until liquid is absorbed.

NOTE: Other herbs may be substituted for the thyme. Try oregano, rosemary, savory or dill.

"It is recorded that ancient Greeks would chew dill seeds during the interminable speeches of senators to keep themselves awake."
— Robin Howe

GREAT MINDS AT WORK: Historian Athenaeus noted that Greek cooks were accorded the same prestige as philosophers and wise men.

Greek With Gusto!

SOUPS

Soupes

Undeniably, the best known Greek soup is *Avgolemono,* a tasty blend of chicken stock, rice and an egg-lemon sauce that gives it a tantalizingly tart flavor. However, there are other equally flavorsome soups from the Grecian kitchen, many are thick and hearty — complete meals in themselves. Some tried-and-true favorites are *Fassolada* (bean soup), *Kakavia* (fish soup), *Fakies* (lentil soup), *Soupa Voithino* (beef and vegetable soup), *Kreatosoupa* (barley and lamb soup) and *Domatosoupa* (tomato and rice soup). Hearty Greek soups are ideal entrées for lunch or dinner — and just the thing to serve as an impromptu meal for drop-in guests.

BEAN SOUP

Fassolada

MAKES 8 SERVINGS

Here's a peasant soup fit for a king! Serve fassolada with crusty garlic bread, feta, olives, a Greek salad and red wine — a veritable feast.

1 lb.	large lima beans	450 g
	water	
1	large onion, chopped	1
3	carrots, chopped	3
3	celery ribs and tops, chopped	3
4	garlic cloves, minced	4
½ cup	chopped, fresh parsley	125 mL
4 tbsp.	olive oil	60 mL
½ tsp.	sugar	2 mL
2	bay leaves	2
28 oz.	can tomatoes, chopped, with juice	796 mL
6 cups	water	1.5 L
½ cup	red wine	125 mL
1 tsp.	crushed, dry oregano (optional)	5 mL
	salt and pepper	

Wash beans thoroughly and place in a soup pot. Add enough water to cover. Bring to a boil, cover, reduce to a simmer and cook for 1 hour with lid slightly askew. Add additional water if necessary to keep beans covered. Drain water, add the remaining ingredients with the exception of oregano, salt and pepper. Bring to a boil, reduce to a simmer, and cook, covered, for an additional hour. Add oregano, salt and pepper.

NOTES: Instead of lima beans, use white navy, great northern or red kidney beans. (These beans must be soaked overnight prior to using).

ADD TO THE GUSTO! For a more intense flavor, add 2 tbsp. (30 mL) tomato paste.

LENTIL SOUP

Fakies

MAKES 8 - 10 SERVINGS

A thick, flavorsome soup that provides comfort from the very first spoonful. Wonderful any time of the year, but especially good for those cold winter days.

1 lb.	lentils	450 g
10 cups	water	2.5 L
3 tbsp.	olive oil	45 mL
1	large onion, finely chopped	1
6	garlic cloves, minced	6
4	medium carrots, sliced	4
4	celery ribs and tops, chopped	4
⅔ cup	chopped, fresh parsley	150 mL
19 oz.	can tomatoes, chopped, with juice	540 mL
1⅓ cups	water	325 mL
¼ tsp.	sugar	1 mL
3	bay leaves	3
	salt and pepper	
	red wine vinegar	

Wash and drain lentils. Place in a soup pot with 10 cups (2.5 mL) of water. Bring to a boil, reduce to a simmer, cover and cook for 30 minutes. Meanwhile, in a skillet, heat olive oil and sauté onion, garlic, carrots and celery until onion is translucent. Transfer the sautéed vegetables to the lentil pot along with parsley, chopped tomatoes, tomato juice, 1⅓ cups (325 mL) water, sugar and bay leaves. Bring to a boil, cover, reduce to a simmer and cook for an additional hour or until vegetables are tender . Season with salt and pepper. Serve hot.

NOTE: As an an option you may add 2 tsp. (10 mL) of vinegar to each serving.

VEGETABLE SOUP

Hortosoupa

MAKES 8 - 10 SERVINGS

The ultimate vegetarian soup! A happy marriage of onions, leeks and assorted vegetables, topped with croutons. A winner in all seasons.

1 cup	dry lima beans, quick-soaked	250 mL
2	medium onions, chopped	2
3	leeks, chopped	3
3	medium carrots, chopped	3
3	celery ribs with tops, sliced	3
6	small zucchini, sliced	6
1 cup	chopped green beans	250 mL
19 oz.	can tomatoes, chopped, with juice	540 mL
¼ cup	chopped, fresh parsley	50 mL
1 tsp.	crushed, dry thyme	5 mL
2	bay leaves	2
10 cups	water	2.5 L
4 tbsp.	olive oil	60 mL
4 tbsp.	orzo	60 mL
	salt and pepper	
	croutons	

Quick-soak lima beans according to directions below. Put all ingredients, with the exception of orzo, salt, pepper and croutons in a soup pot. Bring to a boil, reduce to a simmer, cover and cook for 1 hour. Add orzo and cook for an additional ½ hour. Season with salt and pepper. Serve hot, topped with croutons.

QUICK-SOAK METHOD FOR BEANS: For each cup of beans, add 3 cups (750 mL) water to saucepan and slowly bring to a boil. Boil gently for 2 minutes. Remove from heat, allow to stand for 60 minutes. Drain and use.

TO PREPARE CROUTONS: Cut day-old bread into ½" (1 cm) cubes. Sauté in olive oil, with minced garlic, over medium-high heat for 2 minutes to coat lightly with oil. Transfer to a baking sheet and bake in a preheated 250°F (120°C) oven for 30 minutes.

See photograph page 69.

AVGOLEMONO SOUP

Soupa Avgolemono
MAKES 6 SERVINGS

The egg-lemon sauce, mixed into the broth just before serving, provides the distinctively tangy flavor in this soup. It's a wholesome and delicious soup and quite easy to make, but follow directions closely to ensure perfect results.

6 cups	**chicken stock, page 141**	**1.5 L**
⅓ cup	**rice or orzo**	**75 mL**
3	**eggs, separated**	**3**
¼ tsp.	**salt**	**1 mL**
¼ cup	**lemon juice**	**50 mL**
	fresh parsley, chopped, for garnish	
	freshly ground pepper	

In a large saucepan, bring chicken stock to a boil. Add rice or orzo slowly to preserve the boil. Stir and simmer, covered, for 15 minutes or until rice is tender. Remove from heat and keep warm. Separate the eggs and beat whites, with salt, until stiff. Add yolks, 1 at a time, and continue to beat, with mixer on lowest setting, until blended. Slowly add the lemon juice, continuing to beat on lowest setting until thoroughly mixed. Continuing to beat, add 1 cup of hot chicken stock slowly to the egg-lemon mixture. Pour the egg-lemon mixture into the reserved stock and heat through, over low heat, stirring constantly, without simmering or boiling, for a few minutes, or until the soup thickens sufficiently to coat a spoon. Ladle into soup bowls, garnish with chopped parsley and freshly ground pepper.

TOMATO RICE SOUP

Domatosoupa

MAKES 6 - 8 SERVINGS

Tomatoes are so basic in Greek cooking that it's only natural to expect they would be used to produce a simple, yet tasty soup such as this.

28 oz.	can tomatoes, chopped, with juice	796 mL
1 cup	finely chopped carrots	250 mL
1 cup	finely chopped celery	250 mL
⅓ cup	chopped, fresh parsley and/or celery leaves	75 mL
1	large onion, chopped	1
6	garlic cloves, minced	6
2 tbsp.	olive oil	30 mL
8 cups	chicken stock, page 141	2 L
⅛ tsp.	cayenne pepper	0.5 mL
	salt and pepper	
½ cup	raw rice	125 mL
	fresh parsley or green onion, chopped, for garnish	

With the exception of the rice and garnishes, put all of the ingredients in a soup pot. Bring to a boil, reduce to a simmer, cover and cook for 45 minutes. Remove from heat and allow to cool slightly. Purée the mixture in a food processor or blender. Return purée to soup pot, bring to boil again, add rice and cook for an additional 16 minutes or until rice is tender. Serve hot, garnished with chopped parsley or green onion.

NOTE: When in season, use 1½ pounds (750 g) fresh tomatoes, blanched, peeled, seeded and chopped. As a special garnish, use fresh basil, dill or mint when available.

NOODLE SOUP

Soupa Fides
MAKES 6 SERVINGS

Fides, also called *Mallia Angelou* (angel hair), is a pasta finer than vermicelli. Other pastas you can use in this recipe are vermicelli, hilopites, stars or tiny rounds.

1	small onion, finely chopped	1
2 tbsp.	olive oil	30 mL
8 cups	chicken stock, page 141	2 L
4	rolls fide noodles (½ of 250 g pkg.) or ½ cup (150 mL) tiny pasta or hilopites	125 g
1	bay leaf	1
	salt and pepper	
	fresh parsley, chopped for garnish	

In a large soup kettle, sauté the onion in oil until soft. Add stock and bring to a boil. Crush noodles into the pot. Add bay leaf, salt and pepper. Bring to a boil again and simmer for 8 minutes or until the noodles are tender. Serve hot, garnished with parsley.

ADD TO THE GUSTO! Fresh herbs provide a nice flavor accent in this soup. Try dill or mint.

"The wise man will do all things right, including the seasoning of soup."
— Anonymous Greek Stoic

POSEIDON'S SOUP

Psarosoupa
MAKES 6 - 8 SERVINGS

Herbed tomato sauce adds a special gusto in this hearty fish soup. It's quick and easy to prepare and a meal in itself. Serve it with crusty bread and a green salad.

¼ cup	olive oil	50 mL
1	medium onion, finely chopped	1
4	garlic cloves, minced	4
1	green bell pepper, diced	1
7 ½ oz.	can tomato sauce	213 mL
1 cup	water	250 mL
1 cup	white wine	250 mL
¼ cup	chopped, fresh parsley	50 mL
1 tsp.	crushed, dry oregano	5 mL
½ tsp.	crushed, dry thyme	2 mL
2	bay leaves	2
	freshly ground pepper	
2 lbs.	fish (halibut, cod, red snapper, or mixture), skinned and cut into 1½" (3.5 cm) pieces	1 kg

Heat olive oil in a deep pan. Sauté onion, garlic and bell pepper until the onion is tender. Add tomato sauce, water, wine, parsley, oregano, thyme, bay leaves, and freshly ground pepper. Cover and simmer for 15 minutes. Add fish and continue to simmer, with lid slightly askew, for another 15 minutes.

OPTIONAL: Boiled potatoes, quartered, may be added to individual servings.

ADD TO THE GUSTO! The people of Corfu make a wonderful peppery fish soup-stew which they call *Bourtheto*. A version of that soup may be made by following the above recipe but omitting the tomato sauce and adding an additional onion, 1 tsp. (5 mL) of paprika and a pinch of cayenne.

FISH SOUP AVGOLEMONO

Psarosoupa Avgolemono

MAKES 6 - 8 SERVINGS

The classic Greek Avgolemono Sauce, added to the fish broth, provides a wonderfully tart flavor which transforms a simple fish and vegetable stew into something quite special.

4 tbsp.	**olive oil**	60 mL
3	**ribs celery, finely chopped**	3
4	**medium carrots, sliced**	4
2	**medium onions, finely chopped**	2
4	**garlic cloves, minced**	4
6	**medium potatoes, peeled and cubed**	6
¼ cup	**chopped, fresh parsley**	50 mL
1	**bay leaf**	1
10 cups	**water**	2.5 L
	salt and pepper	
¼ cup	**rice, parboiled**	50 mL
2 lbs.	**thick, fresh fish fillets (cod, halibut or red snapper)**	1 kg
3	**eggs**	3
1	**lemon, juice of**	1

In a skillet heat the olive oil and sauté the celery, carrots, onions and garlic until onions are translucent. Transfer the sautéed vegetables to a soup pot and add potatoes, parsley, bay leaf, water, salt and pepper. Bring to a boil, reduce to a simmer, cover and cook for 40 minutes. Wash and cut fish into 2" (5 cm) pieces. Add the parboiled rice and fish to the soup pot. Continue to simmer an additional 20 minutes or until the fish flakes. Turn off heat and keep warm on the burner.

TO PREPARE THE EGG-LEMON SAUCE: In a bowl, beat eggs and lemon juice until fluffy. Slowly pour in 1 cup (250 mL) of hot fish stock, taken from the pot, continuing to beat steadily. Add the egg-lemon stock mixture to the fish soup, stirring gently. DO NOT BOIL, or soup will curdle. Heat through, over low heat, stirring frequently, for 5 minutes and serve.

NOTES: Use more or less lemon juice, depending on the degree of tartness desired. TO PARBOIL RICE: Stir rice into 2 cups (500 mL) boiling water, cook uncovered for 5 minutes, drain and use as directed.

GREEK BOUILLABAISSE

Kakavia

MAKES 6 - 8 SERVINGS

KAKAVIA is a wonderful culinary gift from ancient Greece to modern civilization. Greek sailors carried the recipe to Marseille where it was adapted and became known as bouillabaisse.

½ cup	olive oil	125 mL
2	medium onions, finely chopped	2
3	garlic cloves, minced	3
2	celery ribs, diced	2
2	carrots, diced	2
28 oz.	can tomatoes, chopped, with juice or 1½ lbs. (750 g) fresh tomatoes, peeled, seeded and chopped	796 mL
⅓ cup	chopped, fresh parsley	75 mL
½ tsp.	crushed, dry thyme	2 mL
2	bay leaves	2
	salt and pepper	
5 cups	water	1.2 L
½ cup	white wine	125 mL
2 lbs.	mixed fish fillets (such as cod, halibut, red snapper, sea bass, haddock, etc.) skinned and cut into 2" (5 cm) chunks	1 kg
½ lb.	shrimp, peeled and deveined	250 g
½ lb.	mussels, scrubbed	250 g

Heat olive oil in a soup pot over medium heat. Add onions, garlic, celery and carrots. Sauté until onions are tender. Add the remaining ingredients with the exception of fish, shrimp and mussels. Bring to a boil, reduce to a simmer, cover, and cook for 45 minutes. (You can prepare the recipe up to this point a day or two ahead of time.) Add the fish and simmer for an additional 15 minutes. Add shrimp and mussels. Simmer for an additional 10 minutes. Serve hot with lemon wedges and croutons, page 88, or fresh crusty bread.

ADD TO THE GUSTO! Improvise. Add one or more of the following during the last 10 minutes of cooking: scallops, clams (scrubbed), lobster (cut-up) or crab legs (cracked).

See photograph page 103.

LAMB BARLEY SOUP

Kreatosoupa
MAKES 6 - 8 SERVINGS

Food authorities predict that the cuisine of the future will be marked by a return to simple yet robust peasant-style cookery. This wonderful thick soup typifies that kind of stovetop logic.

3 lbs.	lamb shoulder, cut into cubes, fat removed, or a combination of shoulder, necks and shanks	1.3 kg
9 cups	water	2.2 L
1	medium onion, quartered	1
2	bay leaves	2
	salt and pepper	
½ cup	barley	125 mL
1½ cups	finely chopped onion	375 mL
1 cup	sliced carrots	250 mL
1 cup	sliced celery	250 mL
1 cup	diced turnips	250 mL
⅓ cup	chopped, fresh parsley	75 mL
2 tbsp.	chopped dillweed or 1 tsp. (5 mL) crushed, dry dillweed	30 mL

Place meat in a soup pot and cover with water. Bring to a boil. Skim off the froth as it rises. Add quartered onion, bay leaves, salt, pepper and barley. Bring to a boil, reduce to a simmer, cover, and cook for 1 hour. Remove bones, separate the meat and cut into bite-sized pieces. Return meat to the soup along with chopped onion, carrots, celery, turnips, parsley and dillweed. Simmer for 1 additional hour. Serve with lemon wedges and garlic bread.

BEEF VEGETABLE SOUP

Soupa Voithino
MAKES 10 SERVINGS

Here's a stick-to-your-ribs soup that's a complete meal in itself. A tried-and-true comfort food.

2 lbs.	beef stew meat, cut into 1" (2.5 cm) chunks	1 kg
2 lbs.	beef bones	1 kg
	water	
1	large onion, quartered	1
2	bay leaves	2
1	large onion, finely chopped	1
3	garlic cloves, minced	3
1 cup	sliced carrots	250 mL
1 cup	sliced celery	250 mL
1 cup	diced turnips	250 mL
4 cups	chopped cabbage	1 L
2	red bell peppers, thinly sliced (optional)	2
19 oz.	can tomatoes, chopped, with juice	540 mL
⅔ cup	chopped, fresh parsley	150 mL
⅓ cup	barley	75 mL
1 tsp.	crushed, dry thyme	5 mL
½ tsp.	sugar	2 mL
	lemon wedge stuck with 3 cloves	
	salt and pepper	

Place meat and bones in a large soup pot and add enough water to bring it to a level 1" (2.5 cm) above the meat and bones. Bring to boil, uncovered. Skim off the froth, add quartered onion and bay leaves. Cover and simmer for 1 hour. Add chopped onion, garlic, carrots, celery, turnips, cabbage, red bell peppers, tomatoes, parsley, barley, thyme, sugar and the lemon wedge with cloves. Add additional water if needed. Bring to a boil, reduce to a simmer and cook, with lid partially askew, for 2 hours. Remove bones, season to taste with salt and pepper and serve.

OPTIONAL: Add a boiled potato, quartered, to each serving.

ADD TO THE GUSTO! Add a dollop of yogurt to each bowl and serve with crusty garlic bread.

MEATBALL SOUP

Youvarelakia Soupa Avgolemono
MAKES 6 SERVINGS

Greek Meatball soup mythology: Meat makes it nourishing, egg-lemon makes it soothing and the combination makes it good!

1 lb.	lean ground meat (beef, lamb, veal or chicken)	500 g
1	small onion, minced	1
2	garlic cloves, minced	2
¼ cup	chopped, fresh parsley	50 mL
1 tbsp.	chopped dillweed	15 mL
	or ½ tsp. crushed, dry dillweed	2 mL
	salt and pepper	
1	egg, lightly beaten	1
¼ cup	raw rice	50 mL
5 cups	chicken stock, page 141	1.2 L
1 cup	tomato juice	250 mL
3 tbsp.	butter or margarine	45 mL
⅓ cup	raw rice	75 mL
2	eggs	2
1	lemon, juice of	1
3 tbsp.	water	45 mL

In a bowl, combine meat, onion, garlic, parsley, dillweed, salt, pepper, beaten egg and ¼ cup (50 mL) rice. Knead thoroughly and form into walnut-sized balls. Set aside. In a deep saucepan, combine the stock, tomato juice and butter, bring to a boil, reduce to a simmer. Add ⅓ cup (75 mL) rice and meatballs. Cover and simmer for 45 minutes. PREPARE THE EGG-LEMON SAUCE: In a bowl, beat eggs, lemon juice and water with an electric mixer until fluffy. Remove 1 cup (250 mL) of hot stock from the soup and slowly add it to the egg-lemon sauce, beating continuously. Pour egg-lemon mixture into the soup, shake pan to combine, heat through over low heat without boiling, for 5 minutes and serve.

NOTE: Meatballs may be prepared in advance and refrigerated. For a different flavor, substitute mint or oregano for dillweed.

*In the olden days, Greek fishermen
used lanterns on their boats to
attract fish at night and to ward off
"Monsters of the Deep".*

Greek With Gusto!

SEAFOOD
Psarika

Greece is blessed with thousands of miles of shoreline and hundreds of beautiful islands. Not surprisingly, Greeks love seafood and take great delight in preparing it. Methods of preparing fish and other seafood vary from broiling with lemon and oil, baking, as in *Plaki* style, braising in tomato sauce, to poaching and frying. If he were mortal, Poseidon — the mythological ruler of the sea — would remind us that the tastiest seafood cuisine is always that which is made from a fresh catch.

BAKED FISH PLAKI

Psari Plaki
MAKES 6 - 8 SERVINGS

Here's a memorable feast waiting to be cooked. *Plaki* refers to the fine balance of fish, herbs, onion and tomato sauce. Very simple and very good!

2 lbs.	thick fish fillets (halibut, red snapper, cod, etc.)	1 kg
½	lemon, juice of	½
	salt and pepper	
2 tbsp.	olive oil	30 mL
2	medium onions, finely chopped	2
2	garlic cloves, minced	2
5 ½ oz.	can tomato paste	156 mL
1 cup	water	250 mL
1 cup	white wine	250 mL
⅓ cup	chopped, fresh parsley	75 mL
2	bay leaves	2
¼ tsp.	sugar	1 mL
2 tsp.	crushed, dry oregano	10 mL
½ tsp.	crushed, dry thyme	2 mL
3	tomatoes, sliced	3
1	lemon, thinly sliced	1

Cut the fish into serving pieces. Sprinkle with lemon juice, salt and pepper and place in a shallow casserole. Set aside.

TO PREPARE THE SAUCE: Heat oil over medium-high heat. Add onions and garlic. Sauté until onions are translucent. Stir in tomato paste, water, wine, parsley, bay leaves, sugar, oregano and thyme. Cover partially and simmer for 30 minutes. Pour sauce over fish. Top with tomato and lemon slices. Bake, uncovered, in a preheated 375°F (190°C) oven for 30 minutes or until fish flakes.

ADD TO THE GUSTO! For extra flair, garnish the dish with pieces of feta and sweet pickled peppers.

BAKED FISH SPETSAI

Psari Spetsiotiko
MAKES 6 - 8 SERVINGS

From the tavernas on the island of Spetsai comes this heavenly recipe for lovers of seafood. Its crusty topping and zesty flavor make this a truly unique Greek casserole.

2 lbs.	thick fish fillets (cod, halibut, snapper, haddock, mullet, etc.) cut into serving portions	1 kg
1	lemon, juice of	1
	salt and pepper	
2 cups	canned crushed tomatoes	500 mL
1 cup	white wine	250 mL
½ cup	olive oil	125 mL
5	garlic cloves, minced	5
½ tsp.	sugar	2 mL
	freshly ground pepper	
	bread crumbs	
1 cup	chopped, fresh parsley	250 mL

Wash fish, pat dry, and place in a shallow baking dish. Sprinkle with lemon juice, salt and pepper. Set aside.

TO PREPARE THE SAUCE: Combine tomatoes, wine, oil, garlic, sugar and freshly ground pepper in a saucepan and simmer for 20 minutes. Sprinkle fish with a layer of bread crumbs, following with a layer of parsley and sauce. Repeat. End with a layer of bread crumbs. Bake, uncovered, in a 350°F (180°C) oven for 45 minutes.

TO MAKE BREAD CRUMBS: Slice French bread thinly. Place on a baking sheet. Bake in a 350°F (180°C) oven for 10 minutes or until crisp and golden. Cool. Process in blender or food processor.

FISH SOUVLAKI

Xifias Souvlakia
MAKES 6 SERVINGS

With the first bite, you'll be whisked away in a flight of fancy to a Greek taverna on a sun-drenched Aegean isle. Chunks of marinated fish, skewered with bell pepper and cherry tomatoes are cooked under the broiler or on the barbecue. Try Swordfish Souvlaki, it's especially good.

1	lemon, juice of	1
⅓ cup	olive oil	75 mL
½ tsp.	crushed, dry thyme or oregano	2 mL
2	garlic cloves, crushed through a press	2
	salt and pepper	
2 lbs.	fish (swordfish, halibut, cod, snapper, rockfish, or a mixture of any firm-fleshed fish), cubed	1 kg
	cherry tomatoes	
1	green bell pepper, cut in pieces	1

Combine lemon juice, olive oil, thyme or oregano, garlic, salt and pepper in a bowl. Whisk briskly. Marinate the fish cubes in the sauce for a few minutes, then thread on oiled skewers, alternating fish with cherry tomatoes and bell peppers. Broil for 5 minutes on each side, basting frequently with the marinade. Serve the broiled kebabs with rice or crusty bread, a Greek salad and Retsina.

See photograph opposite.

SEAFOOD —

FISH WITH VEGETABLES

Psari Tourlou
MAKES 6 SERVINGS

Y ou're about to be hooked! Fish baked like this, the Greek way — on a bed of fresh vegetables accented with garlic, oregano and other herbs — is a feast that's virtually irresistible.

1	medium eggplant, diced	1
1 tbsp.	salt	15 mL
¾ cup	olive oil	175 mL
1	large onion, chopped	1
5	green onions, chopped	5
2	garlic cloves, minced	2
1	green pepper, cut into strips	1
2	potatoes, halved and sliced	2
3	zucchini, thickly sliced	3
2 tbsp.	chopped, fresh parsley	30 mL
1	bay leaf	1
1 tbsp.	crushed, dry oregano	15 mL
	salt and pepper	
1½ cups	water	375 mL
2 lbs.	thick fish fillets (snapper, cod, halibut, bass, etc.)	1 kg
2 tbsp.	butter	30 mL

Peel, slice and dice eggplant into 1" (2.5 cm) cubes. Sprinkle with salt, place in a colander and drain for ½ hour. In a large sauté pan or skillet, add oil as required, and in small batches sauté the onions, garlic, green pepper, potatoes, zucchini and eggplant for a few minutes. Place the sautéed vegetables in a shallow casserole or baking pan. Add parsley, bay leaf, oregano, salt, pepper and water. Bake, uncovered, in a preheated 350°F (180°C) oven for 30 minutes.

Wash fish fillets, pat dry, sprinkle with salt and pepper and place on top of the vegetables. Dot fish with butter, cover with lemon slices and bake, uncovered, for 45 minutes in a 350°F (180°C) oven.

NOTE: Other than oregano, try some of these alternate flavors for fish: dillweed, fennel, basil, thyme, rosemary or tarragon.

PAN-FRIED SMELTS

Marithes Tiganites

MAKES 4 SERVINGS

These tiny fish — called MARITHES in Greek — are delicious as an appetizer, snack or as a main course.

2 lbs.	**smelts, about 3 dozen**	**1 kg**
1 cup	**flour**	**250 mL**
	salt and pepper	
½ cup	**olive oil**	**125 mL**

Clean, wash and dry fish, leaving heads and tails intact. Dredge in flour seasoned with salt and pepper. Heat the olive oil in a frying pan and fry quickly, a few at a time, until golden brown. Drain on paper towel. Serve hot with lemon wedges and Greek Garlic Sauce *(Skordalia)* or Lemon-Oil Dressing *(Ladolemono)*, see page 138.

NOTE: Here's an alternate way of preparing and cooking this recipe: Dip smelts in beaten egg, dredge in seasoned bread crumbs, and place on a greased baking sheet. Dot with butter and broil for 4 minutes on each side.

TRIVIA QUESTION: Are you an ICHTYOPHAGIST?
Answer "yes", if you love seafood.

SEAFOOD SOUFFLÉ

Thalassino Soufflé
MAKES 4 SERVINGS

Light as a feather, this entrée may be served either as a side dish or as a main course for two.

3 tbsp.	butter or margarine	45 mL
4 tbsp.	flour	60 mL
1 cup	hot skim milk	250 mL
4	egg yolks, lightly beaten	4
2 tsp.	lemon zest	10 mL
6	green onions, finely chopped	6
1 tbsp.	chopped dillweed or ½ tsp. (2 mL) crushed, dry dillweed	15 mL
	salt and pepper	
8 oz.	crab, flaked	250 g
6	egg whites	6

Melt the butter or margarine, in a saucepan, over low heat. Add flour and mix well. Add hot milk, stirring constantly with a wire whisk. Cook over low heat for a minute or two. Remove from heat and stir in beaten yolks, lemon zest, green onions, dillweed, salt, pepper and crab. Set aside to cool. Beat the egg whites until they hold a stiff peak. Do not overbeat. Stir 2 tbsp. (30 mL) of the beaten whites into the cooled mixture. Gently fold in the remaining whites with a rubber spatula. Pour into a lightly buttered, high-sided casserole or soufflé dish. Bake in a preheated 375°F (190°C) oven for 35 minutes or until the soufflé rises fully and is golden brown. Serve immediately.

NOTE: For a variation, substitute chopped shrimp, scallops or canned salmon for crab.

SHRIMP WITH FETA

Garides Youvetsi
MAKES 4 SERVINGS

Shrimp and feta are wonderfully matched in this oven-baked dish. It's much like those famous and delicious shrimp entrées you'd get in the colorful outdoor tavernas in the Port of Piraeus.

1 lb.	medium or large shrimp	500 g
1 tbsp.	lemon juice	15 mL
3 cups	Greek Tomato Sauce II, page 139	750 mL
1 cup	crumbled feta	250 mL
½ cup	grated Parmesan	125 mL

Peel and devein shrimp. Wash, pat dry, and sprinkle with lemon juice. Divide shrimp and place into 4 individual casseroles. Spoon tomato sauce over the shrimp in each dish. Top with crumbled feta, followed by a sprinkling of Parmesan. Bake, uncovered in a pre-heated 400°F (200°C) oven for 15 minutes, or until cheese is bubbly.

NOTE: Since feta and tomato sauce both contain salt, it is omitted from the recipe.

ADD TO THE GUSTO! Add 1 tbsp. (15 mL) ouzo or brandy to the tomato sauce before spooning it over the shrimp.

The sight of men sitting at outdoor cafes, leisurely sipping ouzo and playing with KOMBOLOI (worry beads) is common in Greece. It is said that worry beads provide amusement, relieve stress, drive off the "evil eye" . . . and psychiatrists.

FRIED SQUID

Kalamarakia Tiganita
MAKES 4 SERVINGS

The delicate flavor of squid is a pleasure to savor and has been a popular food in Greece for centuries.

2 lbs.	small squid	1 kg
	flour	
	salt and pepper	
	olive oil	
	oregano, crushed, dry	
	lemon juice	

Clean squid, according to directions below, and pat dry. Dredge squid and tentacles in flour seasoned with salt and pepper. Heat about ½" (1 cm) of oil in a deep skillet and fry squid, a few at a time on both sides, along with tentacles, until light brown, about 3 minutes. Drain on paper towels, transfer to a warm serving dish sprinkle with oregano and garnish with lemon wedges. Serve immediately. *(Skordalia)*, Greek Garlic Sauce, page 138, makes a wonderful accompaniment.

NOTE: Heat oil only until a drop of water sizzles but does not spatter. Oil should not smoke.

TO CLEAN SQUID: (1) Pull head and body apart. (2) Squeeze out the beak (mouth) and discard. (3) Cut off the tentacles just below the eyes and reserve. (4) Remove and discard the quill. (5) Place squid on a flat surface such as a cutting board and draw the dull side of a knife over it to extrude insides and remove skin. (6) Rinse and pat dry.

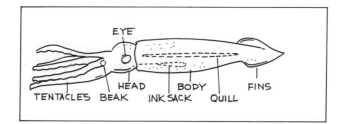

KALAMARAKIA

Kalamarakia Yemista
MAKES 4 SERVINGS

Squid, by any name — Calamari, Kalmar or Kalamarakia — is delicious! In this classic dish, squid is stuffed with rice, pine nuts and currants and baked with tomatoes in an ovenproof casserole. It's wonderful served as a hot dish, but it's equally good served cold.

1½ lbs.	squid	750 g
2 tbsp.	olive oil	30 mL
1	medium onion, finely chopped	1
3	garlic cloves	3
⅓ cup	raw long-grain rice	75 mL
¼ cup	pine nuts	50 mL
¼ cup	currants, pre-soaked in water (optional)	50 mL
½ cup	chopped, fresh parsley	125 mL
¼ cup	chopped mint or 2 tsp. (10 mL) crushed, dry mint	50 mL
	salt and pepper	
½ cup	water	125 mL
2 cups	Greek Tomato Sauce II, page 139	500 mL

Clean and wash squid as directed on page 109. Set aside. TO PREPARE THE STUFFING: In a skillet, heat olive oil and sauté onion and garlic over medium-high heat, until onion is tender but not brown. Add rice, pine nuts, currants, parsley, mint, salt and pepper. Stir, add water and cook for 10 minutes or until most of the liquid is absorbed. Stuff the squid sacks loosely with the filling, allowing some space for the rice to expand. Secure the openings with toothpicks. Place in a greased shallow baking dish along with chopped tentacles and set aside. To prepare the sauce, see page 139. Pour the sauce over the squid. Bake in a preheated 300°F (150°C) oven for 1 hour. Serve with lemon wedges.

SQUID NIKOS

Kalamarakia à la Nikos
SERVES 4

Quick and tasty, one, two, three! The squid is sautéed for one minute, simmered for two and savored after three. No wonder great chefs agree that in cooking, as in all the arts, simplicity is a sign of perfection!

2 lbs.	squid, cleaned, skinned and cut into ¼" (5 mm) rings, including tentacles, chopped	1 kg
4 tbsp.	olive oil	60 mL
1	medium onion, finely chopped	1
3	garlic cloves, minced	3
14 oz.	can tomato sauce	398 mL
¼ cup	chopped, fresh parsley	50 mL
½ cup	white wine	125 mL
½ tsp	sugar	2 mL
1 tsp.	crushed, dry oregano freshly ground pepper	5 mL

Heat 2 tbsp. (30 mL) olive oil in a skillet over medium-high heat. Add onion and garlic. Sauté until onion is tender. Stir in tomato sauce, parsley, wine, sugar, oregano and pepper. Simmer for 5 minutes over medium heat. Remove sauce from skillet and reserve. Wipe skillet dry and heat the remaining 2 tbsp. (30 mL) olive oil over high heat. Add squid and sauté for 1 minute. Return sauce to squid in skillet and simmer slowly, covered, with lid slightly askew, for an additional 2 minutes. Serve immediately with crusty bread.

ADD TO THE GUSTO! A dash of sherry, ouzo or brandy added to the sauce prior to final simmering will provide extra flavor.

In Greek, the words for MAGIC (MAGIA) and COOK (MAGEIROS) sound alike. Is this more than mere coincidence?

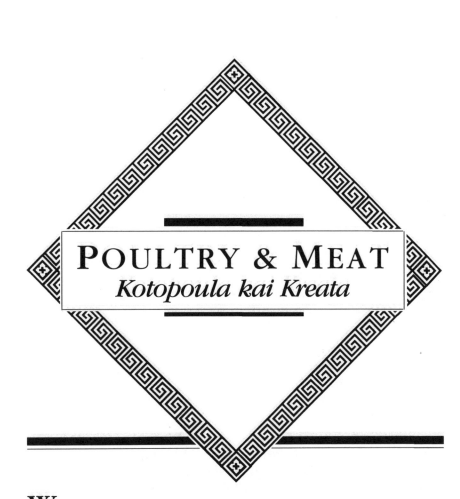

POULTRY & MEAT
Kotopoula kai Kreata

With few exceptions, most Greek meat dishes are prepared in stews and casseroles as one-dish meals. Although lamb is the favorite and most frequently cooked meat in Greek kitchens, poultry, rabbit, beef, pork, and veal are also very popular. These meats are all lovingly prepared in many different ways with herbs and spices for oven and rangetop cooking. Among the classic meat entrees, included in this section, are BAKED LEMON CHICKEN, LAMB AND VEGETABLE FRICASSÉE, STIFADO (stewed meat with onions), CHICKEN AVGOLEMONO (braised chicken with egg-lemon sauce), BRIZOLES (braised lamb or veal chops), MOUSSAKA (layered eggplant and meat sauce casserole), BAKED SPARE RIBS GREEK STYLE, SOUVLAKI (skewered and grilled meat), and ROAST LAMB AND POTATOES.

BAKED LEMON CHICKEN

Kotopoulo Lemonato

MAKES 4 SERVINGS

Something extra special — and very Greek — happens when chicken is flavored with lemon, olive oil and oregano. Here's an easy-to-prepare favorite from the Peloponnese.

3 lb.	chicken, cut up	1.3 kg
2 tbsp.	olive oil	30 mL
1	lemon, juice of	1
3	garlic cloves, minced	3
1 tbsp.	crushed, dry oregano	15 mL
	salt and pepper	
1	medium onion, sliced in wedges	1
5	medium potatoes, quartered	5
8	small carrots, sliced	8
½ cup	water or white wine	125 mL
	salt and pepper	
	melted butter	

Wash chicken, pat dry and place in a bowl. (Skin may be removed from chicken). In another bowl, whisk olive oil, lemon juice, garlic, oregano, salt and pepper. Pour over the chicken. Cover and refrigerate overnight. Transfer chicken to a shallow casserole. Discard marinade. Arrange onion, potatoes and carrots among chicken pieces. Add water or wine. Sprinkle vegetables with salt and pepper. Cover with lid or foil and bake in a preheated 375°F (190°C) oven for 1 hour and 30 minutes. Transfer vegetables to a warm bowl, cover, and keep warm. Brush chicken with butter and place under the broiler for a few minutes to brown.

NOTE: If you don't have time to marinate, mix marinade as above, pour over chicken and vegetables. Proceed as above.

ADD TO THE GUSTO! For a different and delicate anise-like flavor, make TIPSY CHICKEN *(Kotopoulo Methismeno):* Omit garlic and wine. Add 1 oz. (30 mL) Ouzo, plus enough water to make ½ cup (125 mL) of liquid. Proceed as above.

See photograph page 121.

CHICKEN AVGOLEMONO

Kotopoulo Avgolemono
MAKES 6 SERVINGS

A favorite from the lower Greek mainland. When the Greek egg-lemon sauce — *Avgolemono* — is added to fricasséed chicken, it imparts the velvety tartness and the magic which makes this dish so distinctive.

4 tbsp.	olive oil	60 mL
3	whole chicken breasts, halved and skinned	3
1	medium onion, finely chopped	1
½ cup	chopped, fresh parsley	125 mL
2 tbsp.	chopped dillweed or 1 tsp. (5 mL) crushed, dry dillweed	30 mL
2 cups	hot water	500 mL
	salt and pepper	
3	eggs	3
1 tbsp.	flour	15 mL
1	lemon, juice of	1
	hot stock from the stew	

Heat olive oil in a sauté pan and brown chicken over medium heat. Transfer to a platter. Sauté onion in the oil remaining in the pan until onion is tender. Return chicken pieces to the onion mixture in the sauté pan, along with parsley, dillweed, hot water, salt and pepper. Bring to a boil, lower heat and cover. Simmer, with lid slightly askew, for 1 hour or until chicken is tender. Remove chicken from the pan and keep warm in the oven. Keep pan juices hot on the stove.

TO PREPARE AVGOLEMONO SAUCE: Beat the eggs in a bowl with an electric mixer until fluffy. Sprinkle with flour and continue beating. Add lemon juice and beat until blended. With the mixer set on low, continue beating while slowly adding 1 cup (250 mL) of hot pan juices. Return mixture to the stock remaining in the pan. Cook over low heat, stirring constantly for 5 to 10 minutes or until sauce thickens enough to coat spoon. AVOID SIMMERING OR BOILING TO PREVENT CURDLING. Pour over chicken and serve immediately.

SPICY CHICKEN

Kota Kapama
MAKES 4 SERVINGS

Cloves and cinnamon provide a distinctively Greek accent in this tasty chicken stew.

4 tbsp.	olive oil	60 mL
3 lb.	chicken, cut into serving pieces	1.3 kg
2	medium onions, finely chopped	2
3	garlic cloves, minced	3
14 oz.	can tomatoes, chopped, with juice	398 mL
3 tbsp.	tomato paste	45 mL
1 cup	white wine or water	250 mL
1	lemon, juice of	1
½ tsp.	sugar	2 mL
½ tsp.	cinnamon	2 mL
½ tsp.	cloves	2 mL
2	bay leaves	2
	salt and pepper	
	fresh parsley, chopped, for garnish	

Heat olive oil in a sauté pan or a deep-sided skillet over medium heat. Brown the chicken on both sides and transfer to a platter. Add onions and garlic to oil remaining in the pan. Sauté until onions are tender. Stir in tomatoes with juice, tomato paste, wine or water, lemon juice, sugar, cinnamon, cloves, bay leaves, salt and pepper. Return chicken to the pan and simmer, covered, with lid slightly askew, for 1½ hours. Serve with potatoes, rice or pasta and grated cheese. Garnish with parsley.

"Poultry is for the cook what canvas is for the painter."
— Brillat-Savarin

BAKED CORNISH HEN

Kotopoulaki Fournou
MAKES 4 SERVINGS

These Cornish hens, roasted to golden brown perfection, would be appreciated even by the ancient Greeks whose love for game birds is legendary.

2	medium onions, sliced in ¼" (5 mm) rings	2
2	Cornish hens, halved	2
1	lemon, halved	1
¼ cup	melted butter or margarine	50 mL
2 tsp.	crushed, dry oregano	10 mL
½ tsp.	crushed, dry marjoram	2 mL
½ tsp.	crushed, dry thyme	2 mL
	salt and pepper	
1¼ cups	water, white wine or chicken stock	300 mL

Place onion rings in a shallow baking dish approximately 9" x 13" x 2" (23 cm x 33 cm x 5 cm). Rub the hen halves, inside and out, with lemon. Squeeze additional juice over each and place over the onion rings. Brush hens with melted butter or olive oil. In a bowl, combine oregano, marjoram, thyme, salt and pepper. Sprinkle over the birds. Pour water, wine or chicken stock into the pan and place in a preheated 400°F (200°C) oven. Lower heat to 350°F (180°C) and bake for 1¼ hours or until birds are nicely browned. Baste every 15 minutes with pan juices. Add more liquid if necessary. Serve on a bed of bulgur or rice. Spoon pan juices over each serving.

STIFADO

Voithino Stifado
MAKES 8 SERVINGS

Here's a fine recipe for the acclaimed Greek beef stew. Special herbs and spices, along with onions, wine, vinegar and meat are simmered slowly to produce this wonderfully aromatic and flavorsome casserole.

1 cup	red wine	250 mL
2	garlic cloves, minced	2
2 lbs.	beef, chuck or blade, cut into 1½" (4 cm) pieces	1 kg
¼ cup	olive oil	50 mL
2	large onions, coarsely chopped	2
4	garlic cloves, minced	4
14 oz.	can tomatoes, chopped, with juice	398 mL
5 ½ oz.	can tomato paste	156 mL
½ cup	water	125 mL
2 tbsp.	red wine vinegar	30 mL
2 cups	red wine	500 mL
½ cup	currants, soaked in water or wine	125 mL
1 tsp.	grated orange zest	5 mL
2 tbsp.	brown sugar	30 mL
2	bay leaves	2
1½ tsp.	cumin	7 mL
½ tsp.	allspice	2 mL
	salt and pepper	
½ lb.	mushrooms, quartered	250 g
2 tbsp.	olive oil	30 mL

To make the marinade, combine red wine and garlic. Pour the marinade over the meat, cover, and refrigerate for a few hours or overnight. Remove meat from marinade and pat dry. Discard marinade. In a skillet, heat olive oil and lightly brown the meat over medium-high heat. Transfer to a deep pot or Dutch oven. Sauté the onions and garlic in the remaining oil until onions are tender, adding additional oil if necessary. Add the onions and garlic to the meat, along with tomatoes and juice, tomato paste, water, wine vinegar, wine, currants, orange zest, brown sugar, bay leaves, cumin, allspice, salt and pepper. Bring to a boil, cover with a tight-fitting lid, reduce heat to a slow simmer, and cook for 1½ - 2 hours. Or, if desired, transfer to the oven and bake, covered, at 325°F (160°C) for 2 ½ hours, stirring periodically. Sauté mushrooms and add to the stew just before serving.

NOTES: The flavor of Stifado improves after cooking, hence it is a great make-ahead meal. You can prepare it in 2 stages: cook it the first day, add sautéed mushrooms and serve it on the second or third day. This stew freezes exceptionally well. Try doubling the recipe and freezing half, without the mushrooms. It may be kept in the freezer for up to 3 months.

ADD TO THE GUSTO! To make RABBIT STIFADO *(Kounelli Stifado),* substitute rabbit, cut into serving pieces, for the beef. Small pearl onions may be added to stifado ½ hour before cooking is complete or 1 hour if baking. Blanch pearl onions to remove skin and cut a tiny cross at the root end to keep them whole while cooking.

See photograph page 121.

"A good dinner sharpens wit, while it softens the heart."
— *John Doran*

BRAISED VEAL CHOPS

Brizoles
MAKES 4 SERVINGS

For recipes such as this, Greeks have a saying, *"Nani, nani sto tigani"* (Sleep, sleep, in the skillet). The secret to the wonderful taste of this braised veal dish lies in part in the long, slow simmer.

4	**thick veal shoulder chops**	4
	flour for dredging	
1 tsp.	**crushed, dry oregano**	5 mL
	salt and pepper	
4 tbsp.	**olive oil**	60 mL
2 tbsp.	**tomato paste**	30 mL
½ cup	**white wine**	125 mL
2 tbsp.	**lemon juice**	30 mL
1 cup	**tomatoes, blanched, peeled and chopped**	250 mL
4	**garlic cloves, minced**	4
⅓ cup	**chopped, fresh parsley**	75 mL

Trim fat from meat. Dredge in flour seasoned with oregano, salt and pepper. Heat oil in a skillet over high heat and quickly sear the chops on both sides. In a bowl, combine tomato paste, wine, lemon juice, chopped tomato, garlic and parsley. Stir well and pour over the chops. Bring to a boil, reduce heat and simmer, covered, over very low heat for 1¼ hours. Serve with mashed potatoes, rice or pasta.

NOTE: For a variation, use lamb shoulder chops.

POULTRY & MEAT —

PORK AND CELERY

Kapama Hirino me Selino
MAKES 6 - 8 SERVINGS

This classic Greek stew — made with pork and celery — is cooked *Kapama Style,* in a covered pot on the rangetop or in the oven. The pork is beautifully enhanced by the orange zest and herbs.

2 tbsp.	olive oil	30 mL
3 lbs.	pork butt, cut into 1" (2.5 cm) cubes	1.3 kg
2	medium onions, finely chopped	2
3	garlic cloves, minced	3
⅓ cup	tomato paste	75 mL
1½ cups	water	375 mL
1½ cups	red wine	375 mL
⅓ cup	currants, soaked in water	75 mL
1 tbsp.	grated orange zest	15 mL
¾ cup	chopped celery leaves	175 mL
½ tsp.	crushed, dry marjoram	2 mL
2	bay leaves	2
	salt and pepper	
6	celery ribs, halved and cut into 1" (2.5 cm) pieces	6

In a large sauté pan or Dutch oven, heat oil over medium heat and lightly brown the meat. Add onion and garlic and continue to sauté until the onion is translucent. Stir in tomato paste, water, wine, currants, orange zest, celery leaves, marjoram, bay leaves, salt and pepper. Bring to a boil, reduce heat, cover, and simmer gently for 1 hour and 15 minutes. Add celery and simmer for an additional 45 minutes or until pork and celery are tender.

NOTE: Make an even more sumptuous meal by adding 2 or more additional vegetables, such as green beans, peas, okra, sliced zucchini or parboiled potatoes, during the last 45 minutes of cooking.

BAKED SPARERIBS

Plevra Hirinou Fournou

These baby pork ribs are browned, basted, baked....and beautiful! The Greek lemon-oregano sauce gives them a wonderful flavor. Opaa!, They're finger-lickin' good!

BASTING SAUCE:

1 part	lemon juice	1 part
2 parts	olive oil	2 parts
4	garlic cloves, minced or ½ tsp. (2 mL) garlic powder	4
	oregano, crushed, dry	
	salt and pepper	

baby back ribs, allow ½ to ¾ lb. (250-375g) per serving

To prepare basting sauce, combine lemon juice, olive oil, garlic, oregano, salt and pepper in a bowl and beat with a fork. Reserve. Place rib strips in a shallow pan or on a broiler rack. Brown under the broiler, turning frequently to brown well on both sides. When ribs are brown, discard fat that has accumulated on pan bottom. Baste ribs with sauce, place in the center of the oven. Bake at 350°F (180°C) for approximately 45 minutes or until meat is tender, basting and turning the ribs frequently during baking. Serve with hot fluffy rice and a vegetable such as baked squash.

"An Athenian, renowned as a man of taste and for the refined elegance of his table, would have thought his reputation lost had he not offered to his guests ... PORK, considered the delight of the human race."
— Athenaeus

SOUVLAKI

Souvlakia
MAKES 6 SERVINGS

The tantalizing aroma of meat kabobs grilled over charcoal is simply irresistible! Marinate the meat for a few hours or overnight to further improve the flavor. Add vegetables to the skewers and you have the makings of a complete meal.

MARINADE:

½ cup	olive oil	125 mL
1 cup	red wine	250 mL
1	lemon, juice of	1
2	garlic cloves, minced	2
2 tsp.	crushed, dry oregano	10 mL
	salt and pepper	
3 lbs.	lean meat, (lamb, pork, beef or chicken) cut into 1" (2.5 cm) cubes	1.3 kg
	green bell peppers, cut up	
	tomatoes, quartered	
	mushrooms	
	lemon wedges	

Mix ingredients for the marinade in a glass bowl. Add meat and marinate, covered, for 3 hours or overnight in the refrigerator. Thread the meat on oiled metal skewers or bamboo skewers that have been soaked in water. Thread vegetables on separate skewers or alternate with meat. Broil or barbecue 6" (15 cm) from the source of heat, turning once, and brushing with the marinade. Broil 3-5 minutes per side, depending on desired degree of doneness. Sprinkle with oregano and serve with lemon wedges.

See photograph on front cover.

MOUSSAKA

Moussakas

MAKES 10 - 12 SERVINGS

MOUSSAKA is a luxurious one-dish Greek casserole that always gets rave reviews. Layered with eggplant and meat sauce and topped with a thick custard sauce, it's loaded with goodness and nutritional value.

3	medium eggplants	3
	salt	
½ cup	olive oil	125 mL

MEAT SAUCE:

3 tbsp.	olive oil	45 mL
1	large onion, finely chopped	1
4	garlic cloves, minced	4
2 lbs.	lean ground beef or lamb	1 kg
5 ½ oz.	can tomato paste	156 mL
1 cup	red wine	250 mL
2 cups	water	500 mL
½ cup	chopped, fresh parsley	125 mL
¼ tsp.	sugar	1 mL
½ tsp.	cinnamon	2 mL
½ tsp.	grated nutmeg	2 mL
	salt and pepper	
2	egg whites	2
1 cup	grated kefalotiri or Parmesan cheese	250 mL
½ cup	bread crumbs	125 mL

CUSTARD TOPPING:

4	eggs	4
½ cup	flour	125 mL
2 cups	cold milk	500 mL
2 cups	hot milk	500 mL
½ tsp.	grated nutmeg	2 mL
	salt and pepper	
	extra grated cheese for sprinkling	

MOUSSAKA

Continued

Slice eggplant lengthways into ½" (1 cm) slices. Sprinkle with salt and stack with paper toweling between layers. Weight down with a plate and allow to drain for 30 minutes.

TO PREPARE THE MEAT SAUCE: Heat oil in a large skillet over medium-high heat. Sauté onion and garlic until onion is tender. Add meat and continue to sauté until meat is lightly browned. Stir in tomato paste, wine, water, parsley, sugar, cinnamon, nutmeg, salt and pepper. Simmer, uncovered, for 30 minutes or until most of the liquid is absorbed. Remove from heat and allow to cool. Stir in egg whites, cheese, half the bread crumbs and set aside. Rinse eggplant slices, pat dry, and brush with olive oil. Place on a baking sheet and brown on both sides under the broiler.

TO PREPARE THE CUSTARD TOPPING: Beat eggs in a large saucepan. Add flour gradually, beating continuously until smooth. Stir in cold milk. Slowly add hot milk, stirring constantly. Cook over medium heat stirring constantly with a wire whisk, for 10 to 15 minutes or until mixture is thick. Remove from heat, stir in nutmeg, salt and pepper. Set aside.

TO ASSEMBLE: Lightly grease a casserole measuring about 9" x 12" x 2 ½" (23 cm x 30 cm x 6 cm). Sprinkle the bottom with remaining bread crumbs. Arrange a layer of eggplant over the bread crumbs, cover with half the meat sauce, sprinkle with cheese. Put down another layer of eggplant, cover with remaining meat sauce, and another sprinkling of cheese. End with a final layer of eggplant. Pour the custard sauce over the top, sprinkle with a final layer of cheese. Bake in a preheated 350°F (180°C) oven for 45 minutes or until the top turns golden brown. Remove from oven, allow to set for 10 minutes. Cut into squares for individual servings.

ADD TO THE GUSTO! Sliced zucchini and/or potatoes may be alternated with eggplant slices. Cut zucchini into ½" (1 cm) slices, potatoes into ¼" (5 mm) slices. Brush with oil and broil lightly before assembling the Moussaka.

See photograph page 121.

LAMB AND EGGPLANT

Arni Melitzanes Fournoü
MAKES 4 - 6 SERVINGS

Sublime and simple! A typically Greek way of baking lamb with eggplant and potatoes to create an enjoyable and appetizing meal.

1	large eggplant	1
	salt	
2 lbs.	lamb shoulder	1 kg
1	medium onion, chopped	1
2	garlic cloves, minced	2
2 tbsp.	olive oil	30 mL
7 ½ oz.	can tomato sauce	213 mL
½ cup	water	125 mL
2	large potatoes, peeled and cubed	2
¼ tsp.	crushed, dry oregano	1 mL
1 tsp.	crushed, dry mint	5 mL
	salt and pepper	
2 tbsp.	butter or margarine	30 mL

Peel and cube eggplant. Sprinkle with salt and allow to drain in colander for 1 hour. Trim fat from lamb and cut into 1" (2.5 cm) pieces. In a roaster, toss lamb with onion, garlic, olive oil, tomato sauce and water. Cover tightly and bake in a preheated 375°F (190°C) oven for 1 hour. Rinse eggplant, pat dry and add to meat along with potatoes, oregano, mint, salt, pepper and butter. Cover and bake an additional 45 minutes or until meat and vegetables are tender.

"The right blend of spices can be a catalyst, a magic powder, capable of transforming plain food into exhilarating cuisine."
— Marcia Kiesel

ROAST LAMB

Arni Psito me Patates
MAKES 6 SERVINGS

Ah, roast leg of lamb with potatoes — a meal fit for gods and mortals alike! This traditional Greek feast is usually prepared on Sundays, holidays and special occasions.

5 to 6 lb.	leg of lamb	2.5 kg
5	garlic cloves, slivered	5
4 tbsp.	olive oil	60 mL
1	lemon, juice of	1
1 tbsp.	crushed, dry oregano	15 mL
	salt and freshly ground pepper	
1 cup	hot water	250 mL
1 cup	red wine	250 mL
6	medium potatoes, peeled and cut into wedges	6
	salt and pepper	
	oil for drizzling	

Remove lamb from refrigerator and allow to come to room temperature. Preheat oven to 400°F (200°C). Remove excess fell (papery outer covering) from lamb, wash and dry thoroughly. Make several incisions on both top and bottom of lamb and insert garlic slivers. Rub lamb with olive oil and place it, fat side up, in a roasting pan. Squeeze lemon juice over lamb, sprinkle generously with oregano, salt and freshly ground pepper. Place in the center of the oven and roast at 400°F (200°C) for 45 minutes. Lower heat to 325°F (160°C), add hot water and wine. Continue roasting, allowing 30-35 minutes per pound of lamb. For very well done lamb, roast for the longer period. Place potato wedges around the lamb for the last 1½ hours of roasting or until fork tender. Sprinkle potatoes with salt and pepper and drizzle with additional olive oil, to ensure crisp browning. Baste meat and potatoes frequently during roasting. Transfer meat to a warm platter, cover loosely with foil and allow to rest 15 minutes before slicing.

TO MAKE GRAVY: Add 1 cup (250 mL) water to pan juices and deglaze pan. Skim off fat. Spoon some pan juice into a cup, stir in 1 tbsp. (15 mL) flour and whisk the mixture into the pan juices. Stir over medium-high heat until thickened, season with salt and pepper and pour into heated sauceboat.

LAMB AND SPINACH

Arni Spanaki Avgolemono
MAKES 6 SERVINGS

Glorious Greek lamb stews! These noble fricassées, made of cut-up pieces of lamb, call for quick-searing of meat in a skillet, then slow simmering in liquid such as water, wine or stock for about 2 hours or until the meat is tender. A vegetable is added during the last half hour of cooking. In this recipe, lamb, spinach and dill are combined to produce a gratifying meal. Avgolemono Sauce is added just before serving.

3 tbsp.	olive oil	45 mL
3 lbs.	lamb, lean shoulder, cut into 1½" (4 cm) cubes, and/or necks or shanks	1.3 kg
2	medium onions, finely chopped	2
3	garlic cloves, minced	3
1 cup	water	250 mL
1 cup	white wine	250 mL
2 tbsp.	chopped dillweed or 1 tsp. (5 mL) crushed, dry dillweed	30 mL
	salt and pepper	
2	bunches fresh spinach	2
¼ cup	raw rice	50 mL

AVGOLEMONO SAUCE:

3	eggs	3
1 tbsp.	flour	15 mL
1	lemon, juice of	1
	hot stock from the stew	

Trim excess fat from meat. In a skillet, heat oil and sear the meat, until lightly browned. Add onions and garlic, continue to sauté until the onions are translucent. Stir in water, wine, dillweed, salt and pepper. Bring to a boil, reduce to a simmer, cover, and cook, with lid slightly askew, for 2 hours or until meat is tender. Add more water if required. Wash spinach, remove tough stalks and tear larger leaves into pieces. Add spinach and rice to the stew. Continue cooking for 15 to 20 minutes or until rice is tender. Turn off heat but allow stew to remain on burner to keep warm.

LAMB AND SPINACH

Continued

TO PREPARE AVGOLEMONO SAUCE: Beat eggs lightly in a bowl. Sprinkle with flour and continue beating. Add lemon juice and beat until blended. With the mixer set on low, continue beating while slowly adding the hot stock from the pan. Pour the egg-lemon sauce over the meat and vegetables in the pan. Stir gently and heat through over very low heat for about 3 minutes. DO NOT SIMMER OR BOIL OR SAUCE WILL CURDLE. Serve immediately.

NOTE: Use more or less lemon juice, depending on the degree of tartness desired.

ADD TO THE GUSTO! For a variation, make LAMB FRICASSÉE AVGOLEMONO with any of these vegetables:

— CURLY ENDIVE — Same procedure as for spinach.
— ESCAROLE — Same procedure as for spinach.
— LETTUCE — Same procedure as for spinach.
— ARTICHOKES — Add frozen, thawed artichoke hearts, for last 30 minutes of cooking.
— CELERY — Halve celery ribs lengthways, and cut into 1" (2.5 cm) pieces. Add for the last 1½ hours of cooking.
— LEEKS - Wash carefully, halve, cut in 1" (2.5 cm) lengths. Add during last 1½ hours of cooking.
— MUSHROOMS — Sauté in butter or oil. Add to the stew prior to serving.

LAMB AND ZUCCHINI

Arni me Kolokithia
MAKES 6 SERVINGS

This hearty dish is made with zucchini, a fine companion for lamb. The lamb fricassée produces its own zesty sauce as it cooks. It is equally good made with other seasonal vegetables.

3 lbs.	lamb shoulder, cut into pieces	1.3 kg
4 tbsp.	olive oil	60 mL
2	medium onions, finely chopped	2
2	garlic cloves, minced	2
⅓ cup	tomato paste	75 mL
1 cup	water	250 mL
½ cup	red wine	125 mL
⅓ cup	chopped, fresh parsley	75 mL
½ tsp.	crushed, dry oregano	2 mL
¼ tsp.	cinnamon	1 mL
¼ tsp.	sugar	1 mL
	salt and pepper	
4	medium zucchini	4

Trim fat from lamb and cut into 1½" (4 cm) pieces. In a skillet or sauté pan, heat half the olive oil and sauté the meat until lightly browned. Add remaining oil, onions and garlic and continue to sauté until onions are translucent. Stir in tomato paste, water, wine, parsley, oregano, cinnamon, sugar, salt and pepper. Bring to a boil, reduce to a slow simmer, and cook, with lid slightly askew, for 2 hours or until meat is tender. Wash, trim and quarter zucchini lengthways, cut into 3" (7.5 cm) pieces. Parboil or steam zucchini in a covered saucepan for 10 minutes. Add to the stew during the last 15 minutes of cooking. Cool 10 minutes before serving.

ADD TO THE GUSTO! For a variation, make LAMB AND VEGETABLE FRICASSÉE with any of these vegetables:

— GREEN BEANS — Remove ends and strings. Halve lengthways, add to meat and cook for 2 hours.
— EGGPLANT — Peel in alternate strips, cut into 1½" (4 cm) cubes. Add to the stew for last 45 minutes of cooking.
— OKRA — Parboil frozen okra for 10 minutes. Add to stew for last 30 minutes of cooking.
— PEAS — Add peas for the last 15 minutes of cooking.
— POTATOES — Peel and quarter. Add for last hour of cooking.

LAMB IN PHYLLO

Arni Kleftiko
MAKES 4 SERVINGS

Every gastronome loves a surprise! Here's an exotic and fun way to serve a meal that is complete in its own package.

2 tbsp.	olive oil	30 mL
2	garlic cloves, mashed	2
4	thick lamb loin chops, boned and cut into 1" (2.5 cm) pieces	4
12	green onions, chopped	12
9 oz.	pkg. frozen, thawed artichoke hearts	255 g
2 oz.	pimientos, drained	57 mL
	fresh dillweed or mint or pinch of crushed, dry dillweed or mint for each phyllo package	
	freshly ground pepper	
1 lb.	phyllo pastry sheets, thawed	454 g
¾ cup	melted butter	175 mL
	crumbled feta	

Heat olive oil and garlic cloves in a skillet over medium-high heat. Sauté meat for 10 minutes. Add green onions and artichokes and sauté for an additional 3 minutes. Remove from heat, stir in pimientos, dillweed or mint and pepper. Allow to cool.

TO ASSEMBLE PHYLLO PACKAGES: Layer 4 sheets of phyllo pastry, one over the other, brushing each sheet with melted butter. Fold in half, crosswise, brush again with melted butter. Top with one-quarter of the meat-vegetable mixture. Sprinkle with feta. Fold the length of phyllo, both ends, over the center to cover filling. Fold opposite sides towards center, overlapping them slightly to form an envelope. Brush with melted butter and place on an ungreased baking sheet, seam-side down. Repeat the procedure to make 4 packages. Pierce several times with the tip of a knife and sprinkle with a few drops of water. Bake in the center of a preheated 325°F (160°C) oven for 30 minutes. Raise heat to 350°F (180°C) and bake 25 minutes longer. Allow to rest for 10 minutes before serving.

*Did you know that superstitious
Greek cooks make kissing sounds
while preparing EGG-LEMON
SAUCE, "to prevent the sauce from
curdling"?*

SAUCES
Saltses

The best sauce, noted Socrates, is a healthy appetite. The Greek elder statesman was obviously aware that in Greek cooking, sauces are not generally put on top of a dish, but rather, are produced *within* the dish as it is being cooked. Stews and Casseroles, for example, make their own wonderful sauces as they simmer. Simplicity, too, earmarks the Greek's concept of sauce making. Defatted pan juice, with a touch of wine or lemon, is often the only sauce used over many cooked dishes. However, a few sauces used over food are the GREEK CUSTARD SAUCE (for Moussaka and Pastitsio), GREEK TOMATO SAUCE, used with pasta, rice, vegetables, seafood and meats and GARLIC SAUCE, a favorite accompaniment for fried fish, eggplant and zucchini. Orion — one of the 7 sages of the culinary arts — invented white sauce over 2,000 years ago, a sauce which has now become known as Béchamel.

THICK CUSTARD SAUCE

Saltsa Aspri

MAKES ABOUT 4 CUPS

This basic white sauce is often referred to as Béchamel. It is the classic white sauce used to crown Pastitsio and Moussaka.

4	eggs	4
½ cup	flour	125 mL
2 cups	cold milk	500 mL
2 cups	hot milk	500 mL
¼ tsp.	cinnamon	1 mL
½ tsp.	grated nutmeg	2 mL
	salt and pepper	

Beat eggs in a large saucepan. Add flour gradually, beating continuously until smooth. Stir in cold milk. Slowly add hot milk, stirring constantly. Cook over medium heat, stirring constantly with a wire whisk, for 10 to 15 minutes or until mixture is thick. Remove from heat, stir in cinnamon, nutmeg, salt and pepper.

VARIATION: To make a richer version of the custard sauce above.

3 tbsp.	butter or margarine	45 mL
½ cup	flour	125 mL
4 cups	hot milk	1 L
2	egg yolks, beaten	2
1 tsp.	grated nutmeg	5 mL
	salt and pepper	

Melt butter in a saucepan over low heat. Remove from heat. Stir in flour with a wire whisk. Add hot milk, a little at a time, whisking continuously until smooth. Return to medium-low heat and cook, stirring continuously until mixture is thick. Remove from heat, stir in egg yolks, nutmeg, salt and pepper.

EGG-LEMON SAUCE

Saltsa Avgolemono
MAKES ABOUT 2 CUPS

AVGOLEMONO — the best-known Greek sauce — has a velvety texture and a lemony-tart flavor. It is an inspired blend of egg, lemon juice and hot stock.

1½ cups	stock: chicken, fish, lamb or vegetable	375 mL
3	eggs	3
1 tbsp.	flour	15 mL
1	lemon, juice of	1

Heat stock in a saucepan over medium heat. Beat the eggs lightly in a bowl. Sprinkle with flour and continue beating. Add lemon juice and beat until blended. With the mixer set on low, continue beating while slowly adding the hot stock. Cook over low heat, stirring constantly for 5 to 10 minutes, or until sauce thickens enough to coat a spoon. AVOID SIMMERING OR BOILING TO PREVENT CURDLING. Pour sauce over food such as cooked vegetables, dolmadakia, meat, fish or poultry and serve.

NOTE: Use more or less lemon juice, depending on the degree of tartness desired. Refer to page 93 for a thinner variation of Avgolemono Sauce suitable for soups.

BROWNED BUTTER SAUCE

Kafto Voutiro

This simple but satisfying butter sauce is perfect over macaroni or spaghetti. Serve it along with plenty of grated cheese such as mizithra, kefalotiri or Parmesan and freshly ground pepper.

½ lb.	butter	250 g

Melt butter in a saucepan over medium-high heat, watching it closely and stirring frequently. It will foam, then change color from yellow to brown. Remove browned butter sauce from heat before it burns, pour over pasta.

GARLIC SAUCE

Skordalia

MAKES 2 CUPS

SKORDALIA — an inimitable Greek garlic sauce — is great with fried fish and broiled vegetables such as eggplant or zucchini. A wonderful spread for crackers or crusty bread.

5	slices, thickly sliced white bread, crusts removed	5
⅔ cup	water	150 mL
6	garlic cloves, coarsely chopped	6
½ cup	blanched, whole almonds	125 mL
⅓ cup	lemon juice	75 mL
⅔ cup	olive oil	150 mL
	salt	

Cut bread into quarters, place in a bowl and sprinkle with water. Allow to stand for 10 minutes. Combine garlic and almonds in a food processor. Process until fairly smooth. Add bread, lemon juice, olive oil and salt. Continue to process until a thick, creamy consistency is obtained. If necessary, thin with water and/or lemon juice. To thicken, add more bread and process a few seconds longer. Serve chilled.

LEMON-OIL DRESSING

Ladolemono

A wonderful dressing for salads, boiled vegetables and fish, prepared in any manner.

2 parts	olive oil	2 parts
1 part	lemon juice	1 part
	green onion, finely chopped	
	fresh parsley, chopped	
	fresh oregano, or crushed, dry	
	salt and pepper	

Whisk the ingredients together and pour over the entrée.

GREEK TOMATO SAUCE I

Saltsa Domata
MAKES ABOUT 4 CUPS

1	large onion, finely chopped	1
4	garlic cloves, minced	4
2 tbsp.	olive oil	30 mL
½ cup	chopped, fresh parsley	125 mL
1 tsp.	crushed, dry oregano	5 mL
½ tsp.	crushed, dry mint or basil	2 mL
¼ tsp.	cinnamon	1 mL
¼ tsp.	sugar	1 mL
	salt and pepper	
14 oz.	can crushed tomatoes	398 mL
2 tbsp.	tomato paste	30 mL
2 cups	water	500 mL
1 cup	wine	250 mL

In a sauté pan or skillet, sauté onion and garlic in olive oil until onion is soft. Stir in remaining ingredients. Bring to a boil, reduce heat, cover, and simmer slowly, with lid slightly askew, for 45 minutes.

ADD TO THE GUSTO! Add ¼ tsp. (1 mL) allspice and/or nutmeg.

GREEK TOMATO SAUCE II

Saltsa Domata
QUICK-COOK VERSION: MAKES ABOUT 3 CUPS

2 tbsp.	olive oil or butter	30 mL
1	medium onion, finely chopped	1
1	garlic clove, minced	1
1 cup	chopped tomatoes	250 mL
¼ cup	tomato sauce	50 mL
1 cup	white wine	250 mL
	freshly ground pepper	

In a skillet, heat olive oil or butter and sauté onion and garlic until onion is tender. Stir in tomatoes, tomato sauce, wine and freshly ground pepper. Simmer for 15 minutes (or longer if a thicker sauce is desired). Salt is not necessary if using canned tomato sauce.

MEAT SAUCE

Saltsa Kima
MAKES ABOUT 5 CUPS

This is a splendid meat sauce to be served over rice, macaroni, spaghetti and other pasta. Its rich, wonderful flavor comes from the accents of cinnamon, oregano and garlic which are simmered in tomato sauce and ground meat.

3 tbsp.	olive oil	45 mL
1	large onion, chopped	1
3	garlic cloves, minced	3
1 lb.	lean ground beef or lamb	500 g
19 oz.	can tomatoes, chopped, with juice or 2 cups (500 mL) fresh tomatoes, peeled and chopped	540 mL
3 tbsp.	tomato paste	45 mL
⅓ cup	chopped, fresh parsley	75 mL
½ cup	water	125 mL
½ cup	red wine	125 mL
¼ tsp.	sugar	1 mL
½ tsp.	cinnamon	2 mL
1 tsp.	crushed, dry oregano	5 mL
2	bay leaves	2
	salt and pepper	

Heat oil in a skillet, add onion and garlic. Sauté until onion is translucent. Stir in ground meat and continue to sauté until meat is lightly browned. Add remaining ingredients, stir well, bring to a boil and reduce to a simmer. Simmer, covered, with lid partially askew, for 1 hour. Serve over pasta with grated kefalotiri, mizithra or Parmesan.

ADD TO THE GUSTO! Thicken the sauce and use it as a stuffing for zucchini, tomatoes, eggplant or bell peppers. It may also be used as a meat layer for MOUSSAKA and PASTITSIO casseroles. Make it thicker by simply cooking it uncovered for the last 15 minutes which will allow liquids to evaporate.

PAN GRAVY SAUCE

Saltsa

Use the pan drippings of baked or fried meat, poultry or fish.

½ cup	white wine	125 mL
½	lemon, juice of	½
	dash of paprika	
	salt and pepper	

In a bowl, combine and whisk the above ingredients. Remove the cooked meat or fish from the pan. Spoon off most of the fat. Place pan over medium heat and deglaze by pouring in the wine mixture. Cook for about 2 minutes to thicken. Serve over entrée. If pan drippings are sparse, add butter.

CHICKEN STOCK

Kotozoumo

MAKES ABOUT 10 CUPS

Homemade chicken stock is indispensible in Greek cookery. It may be made in quantity and frozen for future use.

2	stewing hens, cut up (4 - 5 lbs.)	2 kg
2	large onions, quartered	2
4	carrots, coarsely chopped	4
4	celery ribs with leaves, chopped	4
2	bay leaves	2
10	peppercorns	10
3 qts.	water	3 L

Rinse chicken and place in stock pot, along with remaining ingredients. Bring to a boil, reduce heat and simmer, covered, over medium-low heat for 2 hours. Skim off froth as it rises. Strain stock into a large container. Refrigerate overnight. Remove congealed fat. Use within 3 days or freeze.

TO MAKE LAMB STOCK: Follow the directions above but use lamb bones and necks, rather than chicken. Simmer for about 4 hours. Add more water if required. Use lamb stock as a substitute for water in recipes such as Youvetsi and Pilaf.

MEDICAL RECIPE: Second century Greek physician Galen prescribed honey as a panacea for "affairs of the heart."

DESSERTS
Zaharoplastiki

There are almost as many wonderful Greek desserts as there are Greek islands, and each dessert is a heavenly experience for the palette. In this section, we present some of the more popular desserts such as *Baklava,* a phyllo-layered honey and nut pastry, *Galaktoboureko,* a custard-filled phyllo, *Rizogalo,* a rice-milk pudding, *Krema Karamelle,* a Greek custard, and *Karithopita,* a tasty and nutritious walnut cake. You'll love all of these — as well as the Greek holiday cookies — such as *Koulourakia* and *Kourambiedes* which are popular any time of the year.

It should be noted that Greeks normally complete their meals with a platter of fresh fruit, nuts, dried fruit, and/or cheeses such as kasseri and graviera. In Greece, it is customary to have sweets as a mid-afternoon refreshment, a late evening snack or as a serving for special occasions.

BAKLAVA

Baklavas
Method: In-the-pan
MAKES ABOUT 50 PIECES

This exotic dessert of Byzantine origin is known and loved throughout the world. It is a nut-filled, honey-saturated, multi-layered phyllo pastry that takes time to prepare. However, the results (and the compliments you'll get) are worth the effort.

FILLING:

2 cups	coarsely chopped pecans	500 mL
1 cup	coarsely chopped walnuts	250 mL
1 cup	coarsely chopped almonds	250 mL
2 tsp.	cinnamon	10 mL

PASTRY:

1 lb.	melted, clarified butter	500 g
1 lb.	phyllo pastry	454 g

SYRUP:

2 cups	white corn syrup	500 mL
1 cup	honey	250 mL
2	orange slices ½" (1 cm) thick	2
1	lemon slice ½" (1 cm) thick	1
1 tsp.	vanilla (optional)	5 mL

TO PREPARE THE SYRUP: Combine corn syrup, honey, orange and lemon slices in a saucepan. Place over medium-low heat for 15 minutes or until honey and syrup make a thin liquid. Do not boil. Squeeze the orange and lemon slices to remove juices and discard rinds. Cool. Stir in vanilla.

TO PREPARE THE FILLING: In a large bowl, mix pecans, walnuts, almonds and cinnamon. To prepare phyllo; allow phyllo to thaw in the refrigerator for 24 hours before using. Remove from the package, unroll, and lay flat on the counter. Cut the phyllo sheets so that they are the exact size of the pan. Cover with a slightly dampened tea towel.

TO ASSEMBLE: Butter the sides and bottom of a shallow, retangular pan approximately 9" x 13" x 2" (23 cm x 33 cm x 5 cm). Place 1 sheet of phyllo on the bottom of the pan. Brush with melted butter. Repeat until 6 pastry sheets have been layered and buttered. Brush the sixth layer with butter and sprinkle with half the nut mixture. Lay an additional 4 phyllo sheets, brushing each with butter. Sprinkle remaining nut mixture on top. Layer 8 additional phyllo sheets over the mixture, buttering each as before. With a sharp knife, cut through the layers of phyllo to make 1" (2.5 cm) squares or diamonds as shown in figure 4, page 22. Brush top with remaining melted butter. Sprinkle lightly with a few drops of water and bake in the center of a preheated 375°F (190°C) oven for 30 minutes. Lower heat to 325°F (160°C) and bake 20 minutes more or until golden brown. Remove from oven and immediately pour half of the cooled syrup over the pastry. After syrup has been absorbed, pour remaining syrup over the top. Allow pastry to rest for several hours at room temperature before serving.

NOTES: To make clarified butter (salt and milk solids removed): In a saucepan, melt butter over medium heat. Skim off and discard foam as it rises. Remove from heat, allow milk solids to settle. Skim off and use clear yellow liquid. For microwave directions, see page 23.

ADD TO THE GUSTO! Baklava, known as *The Sweet of a Thousand Layers,* may be assembled in many ways. Create variations such as these: Sprinkle nuts between each phyllo sheet, between every third sheet, etc. Use almonds, walnuts, pecans, filberts or pistachios, singly or in any combination.

See photograph page 155.

CUSTARD PASTRY

Galaktoboureko
Method: In-the-pan
MAKES 18 SERVINGS

Galaktoboureko — also called *Bougatsa* — is a wonderful milk and honey custard which floats in flaky phyllo pastry.

SYRUP:

2 cups	sugar	500 mL
3 cups	water	750 mL
1	cinnamon stick, 2" (5 cm) piece	1
1	orange or lemon, peel of	1

CUSTARD:

6	egg yolks	6
½ cup	sugar	125 mL
6 cups	hot milk	1.5 L
1 cup	semolina or cream of wheat	250 mL
1 tsp.	vanilla	5 mL

PASTRY:

1 lb.	phyllo sheets	454 g
1 cup	melted, clarified butter	250 mL

TO PREPARE THE SYRUP: In a saucepan, combine sugar, water, cinnamon stick and orange or lemon peel. Bring to a boil, reduce heat and simmer for 30 minutes. Remove from heat and allow to cool.

TO PREPARE THE CUSTARD: In a large saucepan, beat egg yolks and sugar until thick and pale yellow, about 4 minutes. With a wire whisk, stir in hot milk, then the semolina. Cook over low heat for 15 minutes, stirring constantly, until mixture is thick. Remove from heat, stir in vanilla and cool.

TO ASSEMBLE THE PASTRY: Butter a shallow rectangular pan measuring approximately 13" x 9" x 2" (23 cm x 33 cm x 5 cm). Lay one of the phyllo sheets into the pan, allowing excess to extend over the sides. Brush with melted butter, including the parts hanging over the sides. Repeat the process until you have layered about 8 sheets. Spread cooled custard sauce evenly over the phyllo. Fold the hanging edges of phyllo over the custard.

CUSTARD PASTRY

Continued

This will keep it from spilling out during baking. Cut the remaining sheets of phyllo, about 10, to fit the pan. Place them 1 at a time on top, brushing each with melted butter. With a sharp knife, cut through the top 4 layers of phyllo, dividing the pastry into serving portions. See figure 4, page 22. Do not cut through to the custard. Sprinkle top lightly with a few drops of water, and bake in a preheated 350°F (180°C) oven for 1 hour or until golden brown. Remove from oven, slowly pour half the cooled syrup on top. Allow time for the pastry to absorb the syrup, then add remaining syrup. Cool for 4 or 5 hours, uncovered. With a sharp knife, cut through the phyllo to free each serving.

RICE PUDDING

Rizogalo
MAKES 4 - 6 SERVINGS

Creamy delicious! Whether at breakfast, lunch or dinner, this comfort food is always a welcome treat.

⅓ cup	short-grain rice	75 mL
⅓ cup	water	75 mL
⅛ tsp.	salt	0.5 mL
½ cup	sugar	125 mL
4 cups	hot milk	1 L
2	eggs, beaten	2
1 tsp.	vanilla	5 mL
	cinnamon	

In a heavy-bottomed saucepan, combine rice and water. Bring to a boil, lower heat, cover and cook for about 5 minutes or until water is absorbed. Add salt, sugar and milk. Cook over medium-low heat for 40 minutes or until rice is tender. Stir frequently. Remove from heat and cool for 30 minutes at room temperature. Stir 1 cup of lukewarm rice mixture into the beaten eggs. Stir egg mixture into rice mixture in the saucepan. Cook over low heat for 15 minutes or until thick and creamy. Stir in vanilla, pour into individual dishes and sprinkle with cinnamon. Cool, then chill in the refrigerator.

NOTE: A heavy saucepan, or heat diffuser placed over the burner, will help prevent milk from burning.

CARAMEL CUSTARD

Krema Karamelle

MAKES ABOUT 8 - 10 SERVINGS

KREMA KARAMELLE is a velvety custard baked in cups coated with caramelized sugar. After it's baked and chilled, the custard is unmolded and the caramelized sugar — now on top — forms a luscious sauce.

CARAMEL:

1 cup	brown sugar	250 mL

CUSTARD:

2	eggs	2
4	egg yolks	4
1 tsp.	vanilla	5 mL
½ cup	white sugar	125 mL
⅛ tsp.	salt	0.5 mL
4 cups	hot milk	1 L

To prepare caramel, heat sugar slowly in a heavy skillet over medium-low heat for 5 to 10 minutes, stirring constantly, until it becomes syrupy. Pour immediately into warmed, ovenproof custard cups or ramekins. Swirl to coat bottom and sides.

To prepare the custard, whisk eggs, yolks, vanilla, white sugar and salt in a bowl until smooth. Add hot milk in a slow stream, stirring constantly. Skim off froth. Pour into warmed cups. Place in a large baking pan, add enough hot water to the pan to come half way up sides of the custard cups. Bake at 350°F (180°C) for 1 hour or until a knife inserted in the custard comes out clean. Allow custard to cool to room temperature, refrigerate until chilled. Run knife around the inside edge to loosen, invert and unmold on to individual plates.

"For Custard, Cake, and Omelette. No wonder, Child, we prize the hen Whose egg is mightier than the Pen."
— Louis P. de Gouy

WALNUT CAKE

Karithopita

MAKES ABOUT 45 SERVINGS

This nut-filled cake — scented with orange zest and spices and drenched with honey syrup — is nutritious and always welcomed.

½ cup	butter	125 mL
½ cup	sugar	125 mL
8	egg yolks (at room temperature)	8
1 tsp.	vanilla	5 mL
8	egg whites (at room temperature)	8
¼ tsp.	cream of tartar	1 mL
2 ½ cups	cake flour	625 mL
2 tsp.	baking powder	10 mL
½ tsp.	allspice	2 mL
1 tsp.	cinnamon	5 mL
2 ½ cups	finely chopped walnuts	625 mL
1 tbsp.	grated orange zest	15 mL

SYRUP:

1 cup	sugar	250 mL
½ cup	water	125 mL
1 cup	honey	250 mL
¼ tsp.	cinnamon	1 mL
2 tbsp.	lemon juice or brandy	30 mL

Cream butter and sugar thoroughly. Add egg yolks one at a time, beating after each addition until very light. Beat in the vanilla. In another bowl, beat egg whites and cream of tartar until stiff. Gently fold beaten whites into yolk mixture. Combine sifted cake flour, baking powder, allspice and cinnamon with the walnuts and orange zest. Fold into the egg mixture in small batches. Pour into a buttered pan approximately 9" x 13" x 2" (23 cm x 33 cm x 5 cm). Bake in a 350°F (180°C) oven for 30 minutes or until cake springs back when pressed lightly . Remove from oven and cool. Cut into squares or diamonds.

TO PREPARE SYRUP: Combine sugar and water in a saucepan. Cook over medium heat until the liquid "drips in a thread". Add honey, cinnamon and lemon juice. Stir and remove from heat. Pour hot syrup over cooled cake.

GREEK SPONGE CAKE

Pantespani

MAKES ABOUT 45 SQUARES

This recipe will change the way you think about cake. Comprised basically of eggs, sugar, cream of wheat — and a syrup to saturate it when it's done — the cake is light-textured and heavenly sweet.

SYRUP:

1½ cups	brown sugar	375 mL
1½ cups	water	375 mL

CAKE:

8	egg yolks, at room temperature	8
¾ cup	sugar	175 mL
1 tsp.	vanilla	5 mL
1 oz.	brandy (optional)	25 mL
8	egg whites, at room temperature	8
1½ cups	uncooked cream of wheat	375 mL
	cinnamon	

TO PREPARE THE SYRUP: Combine sugar and water in a saucepan and boil gently over medium heat for about 15 minutes or until a thin syrup is formed. Remove from heat and cool.

TO PREPARE THE CAKE: In a bowl, beat the yolks until very light. Beat in sugar gradually until a thick, smooth mixture is achieved. Beat in the vanilla and brandy. In another bowl, beat the egg whites until stiff. Fold half the beaten egg whites into the yolk mixture, alternating with cream of wheat. Gently fold in remaining egg whites. Pour into a buttered rectangular cake pan measuring approximately 9" x 13" x 2" (23 cm x 33 cm x 5 cm). Bake in a preheated 350°F (180°C) oven for 30 minutes. Remove cake from oven and, while still hot, cut into squares or diamond shapes. Pour cooled syrup over the cake, a little at a time, to allow for absorption. Cool, sprinkle with cinnamon and serve.

SHORTBREAD COOKIES

Kourambiedes

MAKES ABOUT 115 COOKIES

These melt-in-your-mouth morsels are special Greek favorites. They grace platters for many festive occasions, particularly Christmas, when they are crowned with a clove, symbolizing the spices brought to the Christ Child by the Wise Men.

2 cups	softened, unsalted butter	500 g
¼ cup	berry (superfine) sugar	50 mL
2	egg yolks	2
1	orange, zest of, finely chopped	1
¼ cup	orange juice	50 mL
1 cup	blanched, toasted, finely chopped almonds	250 mL
4 cups	sifted flour	1 L
	icing (confectioner's) sugar	
	whole cloves (optional)	

In a bowl, cream the butter with an electric mixer until very light and fluffy. Gradually add sugar, beating continuously. Beat in egg yolks, orange zest and orange juice. Stir in almonds and 2 cups (500 mL) of flour. Knead in remaining flour by hand, if necessary, using just enough to make a soft dough. Shape into small round balls and place on an ungreased cookie sheet ½" (1 cm) apart. Flatten cookies slightly and bake at 350°F (180°C) for 20 minutes or until golden, but not brown. Cool slightly and place warm cookies on wax paper that has been dusted with icing sugar. Sift additional icing sugar over the cookies. Cool and store. Cookies may be dusted again with icing sugar prior to serving.

ADD TO THE GUSTO! Substitute 1 oz. (30 mL) ouzo and 1 tsp. (5 mL) crushed anise for orange zest and juice.

See photograph page 155.

GREEK COOKIES

Koulourakia

MAKES ABOUT 40 COOKIES

Greek cookies are so tasty! *Mastiha* (Mastic) — an amber-colored resin — is the important ingredient that provides the wonderful distinctive flavor. *Mastiha* is available from Greek grocery stores and import shops.

½ cup	unsalted butter or margarine	125 mL
¾ cup	white sugar	175 mL
1	egg	1
3	egg yolks	3
1 tsp.	ground mastic	5 mL
4-5 cups	flour	1-1.2 L
3 tsp.	baking powder	45 mL
½ cup	milk	125 mL
1	beaten egg (for glaze)	1
	sesame seeds (optional)	

In a large bowl, cream butter with an electric mixer until fluffy. Continue beating and gradually add sugar, egg and egg yolks, beaten together, and mastic. Grind mastic to a powder with a mortar and pestle. Sift flour and baking powder together. Add to the butter mixture, alternating with milk, beginning and ending with the flour. Beat well after each addition. The last cup of flour should be mixed in by hand to form a dough that is slightly sticky but soft and manageable. Knead for a few minutes, then refrigerate for 2 to 3 hours. Bring dough to room temperature 30 minutes before rolling and baking. Break dough into golfball-sized pieces. Roll in your palms, then on a board to form rope-shapes, about 8" (20 cm) long and ½" (1 cm) in diameter. Make thicknesses uniform so that dough will bake evenly. Fold the "ropes" in half, then twist 4 or 5 times. Place on lightly greased cookie sheets, allowing 1½" (4 cm) between them. Brush with beaten egg, sprinkle with sesame seeds. Bake in the upper third of a 375°F (190°C) oven for 15 minutes or until glaze is golden.

ADD TO THE GUSTO! As a variation, make ANISE-FLAVORED KOU-LOURAKIA: Omit mastic. Substitute 1 tsp. (5 mL) crushed anise, 1 tsp. (5 mL) vanilla. Optional: add 2 tbsp. (30 mL) ouzo.

See photograph page 155.

HONEY-SPICE COOKIES

Melomakarona

MAKES ABOUT 60 COOKIES

These spicy honey-soaked cookies — also called *Phoenekia* — have a delicate orange flavor. A great holiday favorite.

1 cup	softened butter or margarine	250 mL
½ cup	berry or icing (confectioner's) sugar	125 mL
1	egg yolk	1
1	orange, zest of, finely chopped	1
1 cup	orange juice	250 mL
5 cups	flour	1.2 L
2 tsp.	baking powder	10 mL
1 tsp.	baking soda	5 mL
¼ tsp.	salt	1 mL
½ tsp.	cinnamon	2 mL
½ tsp.	ground cloves	2 mL
½ tsp.	grated nutmeg	2 mL
1 cup	finely chopped walnuts	250 mL

SYRUP:		
2 cups	honey	500 mL
1 cup	water	250 mL
1	lemon rind	1

In a bowl, cream butter or margarine with an electric beater until fluffy. Continue beating and gradually add sugar and egg yolk. Beat in orange zest and orange juice. Sift 3 cups (750 mL) of the flour with baking powder, baking soda, salt, cinnamon, cloves and nutmeg. Add to the batter gradually, beating after each addition. Begin mixing by hand, adding as much of the remaining flour as required to make a soft dough. If dough is sticky, add more flour. Knead thoroughly on a lightly floured surface. Shape tablespoon-sized (15 mL) pieces of dough into ovals. Arrange on an ungreased baking sheet. Bake in a preheated 350°F (180 °C) oven for 20 minutes or until golden. Cool.

TO PREPARE THE SYRUP: In a saucepan, combine honey, water and lemon rind. Bring to a boil. Lower heat, and maintain a simmer. With a slotted spoon dip cookies into the syrup, remove and sprinkle with finely chopped walnuts. Allow to drain and cool. Store in air tight tins.

FLUTES

Floyeres
Method: Roll-up
MAKES 36 ROLL-UPS

The Greeks call these sweet roll-ups *Floyeres* (flutes) — or *Poura* (cigars). They are a phyllo-wrapped confection with a honey-nut filling, baked and glazed with syrup. Sinfully delicious!

SYRUP:

2 cups	sugar	500 mL
1½ cups	water	375 mL
¼ cup	honey	50 mL
2 tbsp.	lemon juice	30 mL
1	cinnamon stick, 2" (5 cm) piece	1
3	whole cloves	3

FILLING:

1 cup	finely chopped walnuts	250 mL
1 cup	finely chopped almonds	250 mL
1 tsp.	cinnamon	5 mL
¼ tsp.	ground cloves	1 mL
1	egg, beaten	1
1 lb.	phyllo pastry sheets	454 g
1½ cups	melted, clarified butter	375 mL

TO PREPARE SYRUP: Combine syrup ingredients in a saucepan. Bring to a boil over medium heat, stir to dissolve sugar, reduce heat and cook at a slow boil for 15 minutes. Cool, remove cinnamon stick and cloves. TO PREPARE FILLING: In a bowl, combine walnuts, almonds, cinnamon, cloves and egg. Stir in 1 cup (250 mL) of cooled syrup. Mixture should be thick, but not too stiff.

TO ASSEMBLE: Follow directions on page 25 to make the roll-ups. Bake in the center of a 350°F (180°C) oven for 20 minutes, or until golden. Remove from the oven, spoon hot syrup over each roll-up and place on a rack to drain.

ADD TO THE GUSTO! You may substitute peanuts, cashews, filberts or pistachios for the walnuts and almonds.. Also, if desired, add chocolate chips. For a special touch, add 1 tsp. (5 mL) of brandy to the filling.

See photograph opposite.

DESSERTS —

SHREDDED ROLLS

Kataifi

MAKES 18-24 ROLLS

Yes, these pastries do look like shredded wheat biscuits, but after the first bite you'll love the difference! These sweet orange-scented, nut-filled pastries are absolutely ambrosial.

2 cups	coarsely chopped walnuts	500 mL
2 tsp.	cinnamon	10 mL
2 tbsp.	grated orange zest	30 mL
1 tbsp.	brandy (optional)	15 mL
1 lb.	pkg. kataifi shredded dough	454 g
1 cup	melted, clarified butter	250 mL

SYRUP:

2 cups	sugar	500 mL
1½ cups	water	375 mL
¼ cup	honey	50 mL
2 tbsp.	lemon juice	30 mL

TO PREPARE FILLING: In a bowl, mix walnuts, cinnamon, orange zest and brandy.

TO ASSEMBLE: Allow pastry to defrost in the refrigerator overnight. Remove a small amount of kataifi pastry from the package. Loosen the strands and pat flat to make 3" x 5" (7 cm x 13 cm) rectangles. Place 1 tbsp. (15 mL) of the filling at the bottom end of the flattened pastry. Roll up the pastry to enclose the filling and tuck in loose strands at the ends. Repeat the procedure until all of the rolls have been formed. Place in a buttered, shallow baking pan, spaced about ½" (1 cm) apart. Drizzle 1 tbsp. (15 mL) melted butter over each roll. Bake in the center of a preheated 350°F (180°C) oven for 20 minutes or until golden.

TO PREPARE SYRUP: Combine syrup ingredients in a saucepan. Bring to a boil and stir to dissolve sugar. Reduce heat and cook at a slow boil for 15 minutes. Remove from heat and spoon hot syrup over the hot rolls, allowing time for absorption. Repeat. Cover with plastic wrap and a tea towel and allow to rest for 2 hours. Serve pastries at room temperature.

NOTE: Kataifi shredded dough is available from Greek groceries. While working, keep unused dough covered with a slightly damp cloth.

See photograph page 155.

ARCHESTRATUS — acknowledged as the "father of Western gastronomy" — presented to the world the first cookbook circa 300 B.C.

Greek With Gusto!

APPENDIX
Appendix

An old story has it that the Greeks resinated their wine to render it unpalatable to invaders. Apparently their plan backfired because everyone loved it . . . including the Greeks themselves! Aside from Retsina, the famous resinated wine now known the world over, there are many fine unresinated Greek wines available to grace your table. A description of some of the best reds and whites — as well as brandies and liqueurs is included in this section. And because no Greek culinary experience would be complete without Greek coffee (a dark, rich beverage served in demitasse cups) we've included a recipe. We have also included directions for making GREEK BRAIDED BREAD *(Tsoureki).* Finally, a few words about pots and pans and some kitchen hints to ensure successful cooking.

GREEK WINES

The warmth of the Mediterranean sun and the dry, sloping mountainous environment provide Greece with ideal conditions for producing excellent wines. Further blessed by Dionysus — the mythological god of the vine — the wines of Greece are many and varied. Here are some of the best:

WHITE (to be served chilled)
Aphrodite — a dry vintage wine
Demestica — a light, dry table wine
Hymettus — a light, dry table wine
Mantinea — a light, dry wine from the Peloponnesus
Robola — a dry, full-bodied wine
Retsina — a pine resin-flavored wine
St. Helena — a dry, light table wine from the Peloponnesus
Muscat — a sweet dessert wine

ROSÉ (to be served chilled)
Kokkineli — a resin-flavored wine
Rosella — a robust wine from Rhodes
Roditys — a fruity bouquet; good table wine

RED (to be served at room temperature)
Castel Danielis - a vintage wine, full-bodied, fruity bouquet
Mount Ambelos — a smooth, dry table wine
Pendeli — a dry, full-bodied wine
Demestica Red — a fine table wine
Commandaria — a sweet wine
Mavrodaphne — a heavy-bodied sweet dessert wine
Nemean — a dry, rich Peloponnesian wine

BRANDIES
Metaxa (5 star or 7 star)
Achaia Clauss
Cambas VO

LIQUEURS
Ouzo — a popular anise-flavored aperitif.
Mastiha — a pine-flavored liqueur.

GREEK COFFEE

Kafes
MAKES 4 SERVINGS

Greek coffee is made in a small long-handled brass pot called a *Briki* and served in a demitasse cup. It is made plain *(sketos)*, moderately sweet *(metrios)* or very sweet *(glyko)*. It is prepared from Turkish coffee, is very dark and rich , and is meant to be sipped leisurely. When it is made correctly, there will be *kaimaki* (froth) floating on top of the coffee. *Brikis* are available from Greek or ethnic import shops in 2, 4, or 6 demitasse cup sizes. Don't worry if you can't get one, however. A small saucepan will do just fine. Here's how our cousin Eleni, makes Greek coffee:

4 cups	(demitasse-size) water	200 mL
4 tsp.	(heaping) Turkish coffee	40 mL
4 tsp.	sugar	20 mL

Pour water into a *briki* or a small saucepan. Add sugar and coffee. Stir well. Bring to a boil. Remove from heat as soon as it boils up. When the froth settles down, return the coffee pot to the heat and allow it to boil up again. This procedure is repeated 3 times in total. Divide the froth among the demitasse cups, then fill each cup with coffee. See photograph page 33.

❧

"The custom of drinking coffee is attributed to the prior of a convent, who noticing the effect it produced on the goats who fed on it, tried its influence on his monks, in order to keep them awake during the performance of divine service."
— *Alexis Soyer*

❧

GREEK BRAIDED BREAD

Tsoureki

MAKES 3 BRAIDS

This version of *Tsoureki,* the popular Greek bread, is mildly sweet. It's ideal for breakfast, coffee breaks or as an accompaniment for dinner. The bread dough is cut into strips and braided to form attractive loaves.

1 pkg.	active dry yeast	8 g
¼ cup	warm water	50 mL
3 tbsp.	sugar	45 mL
¾ cup	lukewarm milk	175 mL
¼ tsp.	salt	1 mL
¼ cup	melted butter	50 mL
2	eggs, beaten	2
3½ cups	sifted flour	875 mL
	sesame seeds	

In a bowl, dissolve yeast in warm water with 1 tsp. (5 mL) of the sugar. Set aside in a warm spot for 10 - 15 minutes. The yeast mixture should triple in size. Heat milk to lukewarm. Dissolve remaining sugar and salt in the milk. Add melted butter. Stir the milk-butter mixture into the yeast mixture. Be sure it is just lukewarm, not hot, or you will destroy the yeast action. Pour into a large bowl and add half the beaten eggs, stirring to blend. Reserve the other half for glazing. Begin adding flour gradually until a soft dough is formed. When dough becomes stiff, mix with hands and knead thoroughly. Use enough flour to keep dough sticky but manageable with floured or buttered hands. Pat dough with buttered hands and place in a bowl. Cover with plastic wrap and a towel. Set in a warm place for an hour or longer until dough doubles in bulk. Punch down and roll out to approximately ½" (1 cm) thickness. Cut into strips 1" x 10" (2.5 cm x 25 cm). Take 3 strips, press together at top and braid as shown in the illustration. Finish by tucking and pinching ends together on the bottom. Place on lightly greased baking sheets, allowing about 2" (5 cm) between loaves for rising and expanding. Cover with a tea towel and allow to rise in a warm place until just double in bulk. Brush gently with remaining beaten egg. Sprinkle with sesame seeds. Bake in a preheated 350°F (180°C) oven for 25 minutes or until golden.

BRAIDED BREAD

Continued

If necessary, turn loaves and bake an additional 5 minutes to ensure all-over browning. See photograph page 69.

ADD TO THE GUSTO! To make an Easter *kouloura* (ring-shape), form braids and join them to form a large doughnut shape. Place a red hard-boiled egg in the center before the bread rises. To make a sweeter, more festive *tsoureki,* double the amount of sugar and add 1 tbsp. (15 mL) grated orange zest or 1 tsp. (5 mL) of any of the following: cinnamon, crushed anise, or powdered mastic *(mastiha).*

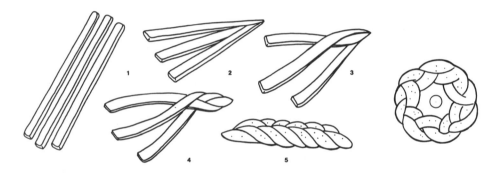

Tsoureki

✎

"The mythological PAN — half man, half goat — taught mortals the art of making bread, say some writers. The name of this food, they claim, furnishes proof. Not so, say others who assert it is in the Greek word PAN (signifying ALL) that we find the real meaning of this nutritious substance; it accompanies ALL other foods, and agrees equally with ALL mankind."
— Cassiodor

✎

POTS AND PANS

Although each recipe in GREEK WITH GUSTO! identifies the required cooking utensils, here is a summary of the pots and pans which are recommended for Greek cookery:

SKILLET: The stainless steel or Teflon-lined skillet is used for sautéeing or frying. Although many Greek recipes are cooked entirely in the skillet, others require the skillet only for preliminary searing or sautéeing. The food is then transferred to deeper pots for stovetop or oven cooking.

SAUTEUSE: The sauteuse (sauté pan) is shaped like a skillet, but is deeper and comes equipped with a tight-fitting lid. Available in stainless steel or calphalon-lining, it is ideal for preparing fricassée recipes wherein the two operations described above are required, i.e., sautéing, followed by long stovetop simmering.

ROASTING PAN: A shallow roasting pan is generally used to roast Greek lamb and other meats. A rack may be employed to hold food above the juices. These pans are usually about 2½" (6 cm) deep and made of enameled steel, aluminum or stainless steel. They allow heat to circulate around the food as it cooks. A usable size is determined by individual needs and the size of your oven. A DEEP OVAL ENAMEL ROASTER, equipped with a domed cover, may be used for cooking poultry or meat and for stovetop poaching.

DUTCH OVEN: Dutch ovens are deep casserole pots equipped with tight-fitting lids. These metal cooking vessels are ideal for cooking foods requiring a long, slow simmer as do Greek stews and soups. A good pot will retain juices and reflect heat inwardly, acting in this respect as a "rangetop oven".

SHALLOW CASSEROLE: Shallow casserole pans are ideal for preparing Moussaka, Pastitsio and other Greek casseroles which require oven baking. They are also used for baking desserts such as Baklava and Greek cakes. Shallow casseroles are made of ovenproof glass, stainless steel, ceramic, and aluminum and available in many sizes. Note that acids in foods such as tomatoes and wine tend to discolor meat and sauces baked in aluminum.

CERAMIC CASSEROLE: Deep ceramic casseroles, equipped with lids, are great for warming food in the microwave. They are also ideal for serving Greek stews, soups and other foods at the table. Use ceramic pots for oven cooking with discretion; avoid those with lead glazing.

GLOSSARY AND GUIDE

— CLARIFIED BUTTER (Butter with salt and milk solids removed): See pages 23, 145.

— FRESH DILL: May be frozen for future use. Wash, dry and place in plastic bags. Place bags inside a sealed plastic container.

— GARLIC PRESS: A useful hand-held device for crushing garlic.

— ORZO: A rice-shaped pasta . Available from Greek groceries or specialty import stores.

— PINE NUTS (pignolis): Small cream-colored nuts from the Stone Pine tree which grows throughout Greece.

— ZEST: The outer, colored, peel of lemon, orange or lime.

— BLANCHING TOMATOES: Immerse tomatoes in boiling water for 2 minutes. Remove, plunge in cold water and then peel off loosened skin.

— DEFATTING SOUP OR STEW: Refrigerate soup or stew overnight. Congealed fat can then be removed easily from the top.

— DEFROST: Defrost foods in the refrigerator overnight, not at room temperature.

— PLANNING FISH SERVINGS: A WHOLE FISH: Yields 1-2 servings per pound or 2-4 servings per kilogram. STEAKS: yield 2-3 servings per pound or 4-6 servings per kilogram. FILLETS: Yield 3-4 servings per pound or 6-8 servings per kilogram.

— FRICASSÉE: A dish of meat browned in oil or butter, simmered gently in a liquid, water, wine, or stock, with vegetables.

— MARINATING: Meats tenderized in wine, vinegar and oil and flavored with garlic, herb and/or spices prior to cooking.

— TO REDUCE USE OF SATURATED FAT: Coat skillet or baking pan with cooking spray, decrease oil in recipes by 1 tbsp. (15 mL).

— SAUTÉ: To fry in oil or butter over high heat, turning frequently and/or shaking the pan.

— TO REMOVE SALT (from feta, grape leaves, tarama) : Soak in cold water for 15 minutes, drain and pat dry before using.

— WHEN NOT TO SALT: Omit salt when using commercial tomato sauce, chicken stock cubes or base, feta, tarama and canned grape leaves.

The astute epicure Brillat-Savarin once remarked, "Tell me what you eat and I'll tell you what you are."

Greek With Gusto!

INDEX

INDEX

INDEX

OLA KALA KAI TO MELI GLYKO
All's well and the honey's sweet!

SHARE GREEK WITH GUSTO! WITH A FRIEND

Please send _____ copies of **GREEK WITH GUSTO!** at $14.95 per book plus $2.00 (total order) for postage and handling.

Number of books _____ x $14.95 = $ _____
Handling charge _____ = $ ____2.00____
After January 1, 1991, if applicable, add G.S.T. tax = $ _____
Total Enclosed _____ = $ _____

Name: _____
Street _____
City: _____ Province/State: _____
Postal/Zip Code: _____

Make cheque or money order payable to :

> JUNIRO ARTS PUBLICATIONS
> 28 Butte Place NW
> Calgary, Alberta, T2L 1P2

American orders please pay in U.S. funds. Price is subject to change. For volume rates for fund raising groups contact Juniro Arts Publications.

SHARE GREEK WITH GUSTO! WITH A FRIEND

Please send _____ copies of **GREEK WITH GUSTO!** at $14.95 per book plus $2.00 (total order) for postage and handling.

Number of books _____ x $14.95 = $ _____
Handling charge _____ = $ ____2.00____
After January 1, 1991, if applicable, add G.S.T. tax = $ _____
Total Enclosed _____ = $ _____

Name: _____
Street _____
City: _____ Province/State: _____
Postal/Zip Code: _____
Make cheque or money order payable to :

> JUNIRO ARTS PUBLICATIONS
> 28 Butte Place NW
> Calgary, Alberta, T2L 1P2

American orders please pay in U.S. funds. Price is subject to change. For volume rates for fund raising groups contact Juniro Arts Publications.